SOCIAL CONSCIENCE IN SANSKRIT LITERATURE

SOCIAL CONSCIENCE IN SANSKRIT LITERATURE

DANIEL JAMES BISGAARD

MOTILAL BANARSIDASS PUBLISHERS
PRIVATE LIMITED • DELHI

First Edition: Delhi, 1994

ISBN: 81-208-1116-x

Also available at:
MOTILAL BANARSIDASS
41 U.A., Bungalow Road, Jawahar Nagar, Delhi 110 007
120 Royapettah High Road, Mylapore, Madras 600 004
16 St. Mark's Road, Bangalore 560 001
Ashok Rajpath, Patna 800 004
Chowk, Varanasi 221 001

PRINTED IN INDIA
BY JAINENDRA PRAKASH JAIN AT SHRI JAINENDRA PRESS, A-45 NARAINA, PHASE I, NEW DELHI 110 028 AND PUBLISHED BY NARENDRA PRAKASH JAIN FOR MOTILAL BANARSIDASS PUBLISHERS PRIVATE LIMITED, BUNGALOW ROAD, DELHI 110 007

CONTENTS

ABBREVIATIONS

Des.	The *Deśopadeśa* of Kṣemendra.
Dvs.	The *Dhūrtaviṭasamvāda* of Īśvaradatta.
Ep. Ind.	*Epigraphia Indica.*
HASL	F. Max Müller's *History of Ancient Sanskrit Literature.*
HOS	The *Harvard Oriental Series.*
HSL	A. B. Keith's *History of Sanskrit Literature.*
HSLCP	S. N. Dasgupta and S. K. De's *History of Sanskrit Literature: Classical Period.*
IHQ	The *Indian Historical Quarterly.*
IIJ	The *Indo-Iranian Journal.*
JA	*Journal Asiatique.*
JAOS	The *Journal of the American Oriental Society.*
JBRAS	The *Journal of the Royal Asiatic Society: Bombay Branch.*
KSTS	The *Kashmir Series of Texts and Studies.*
Mbh.	The *Mahābhārata.*
MS	The *Maitrāyaṇī Saṃhitā.*
N	The *Narmamālā* of Kṣemendra.
NIA	The *New Indian Antiquary.*
Pa.	Pāṇini's *Aṣṭādhyāyī.*
PAPS	The *Proceedings of the American Philosophical Society*
Pp.	The *Padmaprābhṛtaka* of Śūdraka.
Pt.	The *Pādatāḍitaka* of Śyāmilaka.
RSG	J. F. Staal's *Reader on the Sanskrit Grammarians.*
RT	The *Rājataraṅgiṇī* of Kalhaṇa.
SD	A. B. Keith's *The Sanskrit Drama.*
SP	The *Śārṅgadharapaddhati.*
SRB	The *Subhāṣitaratnabhāṇḍāgāram.*
Ubh	The *Ubhayābhisārikā* of Vararuci.
VS	The *Subhāṣitāvalī* of Vallabhadeva.
WHS	S. K. De's "Wit, Humour and Satire in Ancient Indian Literature."
WZKSOA	*Wiener Zeitschrift für des Kunde Sud-und Ostasien.*

INTRODUCTION

Since it takes considerable time and diligence to acquire the skills necessary to read Sanskrit literature, it is fair to ask if the end justifies the means. That the question should arise here, after so many years of study of the language and its literature, may seem peculiar; that the question should arise at all, is not: the achievement of Sanskrit literature has been called in question by various Western and Indian critics for more than a century now. Because this essay is, to a large extent, in response to the objections of these critics, it will be necessary to examine their arguments in some detail. We might briefly summarize their arguments by saying that the critics have considered some of the better known—and most 'artificial'—works of Sanskrit literature and concluded that two factors, Brāhmaṇism and royal patronage, distorted the literature to the extent that it failed to reflect ordinary human experience or to speak to its needs. I think that many of these criticisms are justified with regard to many—but not all—of the better-known Sanskrit classics; yet I do not think these criticisms hold true for the whole range of Sanskrit literature. Here I hope to call attention to other areas of the literature where realism prevails in greater measure. These areas of Sanskrit literature reveal in its authors a social conscience which led them to criticize hypocrisy and injustice within their society while calling attention to the lot of the exploited. But, before rushing headlong into a defense of the authors of Sanskrit literature, let us first consider exactly how their achievement has been impugned.

F. Max-Müller

As long ago as 1859, F. Max-Müller was denouncing what he clearly felt was a pernicious practice of the Brāhmaṇas: their revision of ancient Sanskrit texts in order to better bolster their hierarchical supremacy. Müller wrote that the Brāhmaṇa had imposed the 'fetters of an intellectual tyranny'[1] upon the peoples of India. In explaining the extraordinary success of a solitary reformer, Śākyamuni-buddha, Müller condemned the Brāhmaṇas as follows:[2]

> . . .their caste, as far as we know the history and traditions of India, has always been in reality the ruling caste. Their ministry was courted as the only means of winning divine favour, their doctrines were admitted as infallible. their gods were worshipped as the only true gods, and their voice was powerful enough to stamp the simple strains of the Ṛshis and the absurd lucubrations of the authors of the Brāhmaṇas, with a divine authority.. . . . In order to overthrow one of the oldest religions of the world, it was sufficient that one man should challenge the authority of the Brāhmaṇas, the gods of the earth (Bhūdevas), and preach among the scorned and degraded creatures of God the simple truth that salvation was possible without the mediation of priests, and without a belief in books to which these very priests had given the title of revelation.

Müller went on to argue that the Brāhmaṇas, confronted by epic traditions in clear conflict with Brāhmaṇical law, rewrote the texts in such a way as to minimize that opposition. Thus, though Brāhmaṇic law forbids polyandry, Brāhmaṇa editors rationalized Draupadī's marriage to no less than five husbands by the insertion of a far-fetched anecdote of extreme filial obedience.[3] Müller also found that the expedient of revision was again traceable in the *Rāmāyaṇa* of King Daśaratha's killing of a Brāhmaṇa's; son where the reader's outrage in reaction to such a heinous crime is mollified through having the boy himself explain to his murderer that he is only the son of a Śūdra woman after all.[4] Of course the killing of a Śūdra boy would scandalize no one. One may form an accurate picture of the contempt in which the Brāhmaṇas held the Śūdras by noting along with Müller that later it would be considered a grave sin to recite Vedic hymns in a place where they might be overheard by a Śūdra. This fact presented obvious difficulties in the case of Kavaṣa Ailūṣa, admitted to be both the *ṛṣi* of several Vedic hymns and yet the son of a slave. The *Aitareya-Brāhmaṇa* recounts a story of the priests of a sacrifice horrified to discover Kavaṣa Ailūṣa ready to participate in their rites: "The child of a slave woman, a cheat, no Brāhmaṇa; how has he been consecrated in our midst?" They sent him out to the desert, (saying) "There let thirst slay him; let him drink not the water of the Sarasvatī."[5] The priests later admit the hapless fellow on the grounds that hymns have been revealed to him and he has therefore been extraordinarily favoured by the gods. Along the same lines, Müller cites the story of Kakṣīvat who, though supposedly a Kṣatriya in Vedic legend, accepted a remuneration of the type monopolised by the Brāhmaṇas. As Kakṣīvat was also a *ṛṣi*, it was necessary to explain his transgression away through a later story of his being in fact the son of the *ṛṣi dīrghātamās* all along, and was thus eligible to perform sacrifices and receive *dakṣiṇās*. In both cases Müller has sought to establish that a far less rigid social hierarchy prevailed in the Vedic era, and that the Brāhmaṇas utilized Sanskrit literature to obscure that greater measure of social freedom alluded to in the oldest *śruti*.[6]

A. Berriedale Keith

A little more than two decades after Max-Müller's death, A. B. Keith defended the Brāhmaṇas as 'the source of the intellectual distinction of India,'[7] the producers of Indian philosophy and the Sanskrit drama. Yet after all that, Keith went on to attribute the numerous faults and limitations of the Sanskrit drama precisely to corresponding faults in the Brāhmaṇic outlook. Keith noted that the Brāhmaṇic mind forever created broadly conceived, stereotyped characters and plots totally lacking subtlety, detail, or anything that might pass for realism. The justification for such extreme idealism in dramatic composition was a strong commitment to the production of sentiment in the minds of the audience. It was apparently presupposed that depth of characterization, such as might be found in a hero with faults or in a villain with a single virtue, would somehow introduce unwanted ambivalence in the minds of the audience and would inhibit the development there of that sentiment which the playwright had taken such pains to create with lyric stanzas, music, dance, song, mime and dramatic gestures.[8] Thus, Rāma is represented as a totally transcendent hero with no human characteristics with which one might identify him as man; Rāvaṇa is always a stupid, boastful, pasteboard villain. That the Brāhmaṇas were the inheritors of the epic tradition—as well as those who adapted and modified it to their own ends—resulted in a truly amazing number of dramatic representations of the Rāma story and other popular plots drawn from the epics and created along very similar lines. This led, naturally, to an eclipse of real dramatic structure, let alone suspense. The playwrights devoted themselves to increasingly recondite lyric stanzas and diction, both of which could only have been fully comprehended by a highly educated elite among the audience. Thus the plays move, as Keith characterizes the *Abhijñānaśākuntalam*, 'in a narrow world far removed from the cruelty of real life', where neither the workings of the idealized society depicted nor the significance of the human experience are questioned.[9]

And yet, if Keith believed the Sanskrit drama to reflect the limitations of its Brāhmaṇa creators, he also believed it to share the limitations of its audience. He repeatedly stresses the contrast between the appeal of the classical Greek drama to a wide popular audience on the one hand, and, on the other hand, the narrow audience of the Sanskrit drama composed of Brāhmaṇas, royal patrons and effete 'men about town', the *nāgarakas*.[10] The Brāhmaṇa audience would have enjoyed the recondite diction, word-play and wealth of poetic figures in the decorative lyric stanzas. The royal audience, then, would be expected to take pleasure in the frequent depiction of idealized monarchs, successful in both love and war. For that matter, the numerous plays modelled on the *Mahābhārata* were devoted to the narration of tales of idealized warriors: Rāma and Kṛṣṇa being, of course, *deified* Kṣatriyas. The *nāgarakas*, for their part, would be expected to drink in the beauty, luxury, and romance of the plays. Yet the ideal of romantic love is one of the first things to suffer at the hands of Brāhmaṇa playwrights composing for a royal audience: for, as Keith notes, 'The ideal of a romantic love between two persons, free and independent, masters of their own destinies, is in great measure denied to them, and they are reduced to the benality of the intrigue between the king and the damsel who is destined to be his wife, but who by some accident has been introduced into his harem in a humble position.'[11]

And if Keith found that the generalized impersonality of the drama inhibited the naturalistic depiction of heroism and romance, he was vexed to find that the same idealism created a blandly apathetic outlook among all great Sanskrit poets, and which precluded them from voicing any expression of social discontent. He found the poets to

> live moreover in a world of tranquil calm, not in the sense that sorrow and suffering are unknown, but in the sense that there prevails a rational order in the world which is the outcome not of blind chance but to the actions of man in previous births. Discontent with the constitution of the universe, rebellion against its decrees, are incompatible with the serenity engendered by this recognition by all the Brāhmaṇical poets of the rationality of the world order. Hence we can trace no echo of social discontent; the poets were courtiers who saw nothing whatever unsatisfactory in the life around them.[12]

S. N. Dasgupta and S. K. De

In their own *History of Sanskrit Literature*: *Classical Period*, S. N. Dasgupta and S. K. De acknowledge that their 'indebtedness to Professor Winternitz's German Edition, Vol. III, and Prof. Keith's works, as well as to other Western and Indian scholars, cannot be exaggerated.'[13] Indeed, after reading Keith's works in conjunction with their book it is impossible not to take them at their word; it seems a good many concepts, interpretations, even phrases have been incorporated by Dasgupta and De with no further acknowledgement beyond that of the generalized one just quoted. Nevertheless, Dasgupta and De do, in their long introductory chapters, elaborate upon Keith's judgements in such a way as to warrant inclusion here.

To begin with, Dasgupta does admit that the terms 'artificial' and 'ornate' may fairly be applied to whole periods of Sanskrit literature, but he takes considerable pains to argue that the terms should not in fairness be applied to its whole history. He finds neither the *Rāmāyaṇa* nor the *Mahābhārata* 'artificial', nor Aśvaghoṣa's works 'ornate'.[14] He would apply these terms to the poets 'of a degenerate time, when the poets had to prove themselves as great pundits.'[15] He concludes that this unfortunate trend was the result of two factors. The first factor was the 'stagnating effect' which the *Smṛti* injunctions increasingly imposed upon Indian social and intellectual life.[16] The second factor was conservatism in the Indian perspective which continually resisted the fertilization of foreign cultural influence. Dasgupta, in fact, finds a major reason for the continuity of Indian culture 'in the insular character of our civilization and the extreme doggedness and obstinacy amounting to haughtiness and national pride rising to the level of religion against the conscious acceptance of any contribution from any foreigner.'[17]

Unlike Müller and A. B. Keith, neither Dasgupta nor De directly attribute the admitted shortcomings of Sanskrit literature to corresponding faults in the perspective of its Brāhmaṇa authors with anything approaching candour. To be sure, Dasgupta devotes nearly thirty pages decrying the role of the *Smṛtis* in the 'collapse of the Indian genius in formalistic lines and in artificiality in social customs, behaviours, and actions, in philosophy and in art, . . .naturally reflected in the development of the Sanskrit literature of a later age';[18] but nowhere does he speak directly of the *Smṛtis*' origin in and advancement of the Brāhmaṇa class. We may only speculate whether or not Dasgupta, himself not a Brāhmaṇa, kept silent on this point out of deference to a larger proportion of his countrymen—and an even larger proportion of his academic colleagues! De says nothing on this point. De does, nevertheless, suggest that Sanskrit literature did assume many of its most characteristic artificialities in conjunction with an audience made up of representatives of the following three groups: royal patrons; *nāgarakas* (a subculture of urban dandies); and *rasikas* or *sahṛdayas* (connoisseurs of literary excellence).

De thinks that Sanskrit poetry was fostered by patronage from its very beginning. He therefore finds it natural that this literature 'reflects the graces, as well as the artificialities, of courtly life.'[19] Small wonder then, that he detected in this subsidized literature 'a marked preference of what catches the eye to what touches the heart.'[20]

It was apparently A. B. Keith who first thought to look to Vātsyāyana's *Kāmasūtra* for a description of the citified dandy or *nāgaraka* who as a group apparently formed a significant portion of the Sanskrit author's audience.[21] It seems certain that both Dasgupta and De considered Keith's reference to Vātsyāyana noteworthy, since both imitate it at length in their respective sections of the same book! Although he fails to refer to Keith—(or De, or even Vātsyāyana!)—Dasgupta gives the fullest rendering of this obviously important passage:[22]

> If we wish to picture before our mind the life of a city beau in ancient India we can imagine him as having a house beside a lake with a garden beside it, having many rooms for his works, for meeting people, for sleep and for bath—a house divided into an external and internal part, the internal part for the ladies. His bed is covered with incense, pillowed on both sides, the head and the feet, and very soft in the middle, with a seat for an idol or image of a deity at the headside of the bed, a small table with four legs of the same height as the bed on which there are flower-garlands, sandal-paste, a little wax in a vessel, a little fragrant fan, spices: there is a spitoon on the ground, the 'Vīṇā' is hanging on a peg in the wall; there is [*sic*] a number of pictures hanging in proper positions in the wall, articles for painting on a table, some books of poems and some garlands. The seats in the room are covered with beautiful covers; outside in the verandah there are probably birds in a cage and arrangements of diverse sports in the yard, a swing hanging in a shady place; and an elevated quadrangle for sitting at pleasure.
>
> The beau rises in the morning, performs his morning ablutions, offers his morning prayers and other religious duties, besmears himself faintly with sandal-paste and wears clothes fragrant with the smoke of *aguru*, wears a garland on his hair, slightly paints his lips with red, chews betel leaves, and looking at his face at a mirror, will go out to perform his daily duties. He takes his bath everyday, cleanses his body with perfumes, gets himself massaged, sometimes takes vapour-baths, shaves generally every three days, takes his meals in the middle of the day, in the afternoon and also in the night; after meals he would either play or go to sleep and in the evenings go out to the clubs for sport. The early part of the night may be spent in music and the night in love-making of diverse kinds, receiving ladies and attending to them. He arranges festivities on the occasions of worship of particular gods; in the clubs he talks about literature in small groups, he sits together and drinks, goes out to gardens and indulges in sports. On festive occasions in the temple of

> Sarasvatī dramatic performances are held and actors and dancers from different temples come and meet together for the performance. Guests are received and well attended to. The clubs were generally located in the houses of courtesans or in special houses or in the houses of some members of the club. These clubs were often encouraged by the kings and in such places men more or less of the same age, intelligence, character and riches, met and spent their time in mutual conversation or conversation with courtesans. There they discussed literature, or practiced dramatic art, dancing, singing, etc. They would often drink wine at each other's houses.

From such a description of a typical member of the Sanskrit author's audience, one cannot do better than Keith, who dryly notes 'From such a nature, of course, anything heroic cannot be expected, and the poets recognize this state of affairs; but it demands refinement, beauty, luxury, and the demand is fully met.'[23]

Returning to De's delineation of the three types of men composing the Sanskrit authors' audience, we are left with the final group, the literary connoisseurs, *rasikas* or *sahṛdayas*. These were men of undoubted expertise and refinement of judgement in both the theory and practice of literature; and, as such, often constituted the most demanding section of the Sanskrit authors' audience. It may be assumed that the poets' striving to create increasingly recondite effects was directed to this group's tastes, and it must share the blame for the laboured mannerism which resulted. Further, it follows that poetry directed at this group must have become increasingly divorced from the sentiments of the common people, let alone their capacity to follow it.

Small wonder then that De finds such poetry 'aristocratic' and asserts that it had been so from its very beginnings. De's criticisms of the resultant literature do not quite have the sharp edge one finds in those of Keith. Nevertheless, De does find that the poet writing for such an audience 'is content with the elegant symbols of reality rather than strive for the reality itself; and his work is very often nothing more than a delicate blossom of fancy, fostered in a world of tranquil calm.'[24] And, although

De stops short of Keith's disappointment at hearing 'no echo of social discontent', still he does point to a 'complacent attitude towards life [which] falls in with the view of Sanskrit Poetics which distinguishes the actual world from the world of poetry, where the hard and harsh facts of life dissolve themselves into an imaginative system of pleasing fictions.'[25]

D. D. Kosambi

We have to this point concerned ourselves with relatively fine points of inclusion, exclusion, discretion and emphasis—all of which do little to prepare the reader for the stentorian voice of D. D. Kosambi. Yet, as shrill as that voice sometimes is, still it must be admitted that it often gives expression to some of the most profoundly original insights produced in the last century's study of Sanskrit's literary history. As a Marxist and *nāstika*, Kosambi attacks what he believes to be erroneous suppositions concerning his nation's cultural history with a kind of fury perhaps only found in the alienation of one so dramatically opposed to his cultural mainstream.

The most convenient introduction to Kosambi's thought might well come from a consideration of his demolition of his nation's most popularly revered literary monument, the *Bhagavadgītā* in *Myth and Reality*[26]—and there can be little doubt of which of these two terms Kosambi regards as most descriptive of the *Gītā*.

The vast appeal of the *Gītā*, Kosambi feels, may be explained by its thoroughgoing inconsistency; it quite literally promises all things to all men. He notes that the book is highly equivocal in emphasizing non-violence while at the same time inciting men to the bloodshed of war. Along the same lines, the song's divine singer declares it impossible to slay or be slain, yet later offers a vision of warriors rushing into oblivion through the many portals of his own voracious mouths. Again, the sacred character of the fire-sacrifice is questioned, yet all life is later admitted to depend solely upon the rain it supposedly generates. Kosambi characterizes such equivocation as a 'slippery opportunism' which fosters the same failing in 'so many Gita lovers'.[27] But the book's pernicious effects go further: 'Once it is admitted that material reality is gross illusion, the rest follows quite simply; the world of 'doublethink' is the only one that matters.'[28] If the *Gītā*'s own mutual inconsistencies argue against its acceptance as a valid philosophical text, then we might well ask what its function has been and is today, for Kosambi observes that 'the book has had its uses'.[29]

It does go without saying that such a flexible document as the *Gītā* might be expected to have been often employed by diverse groups for their own class interests, and Kosambi declares this to be the case. But at bottom he found the *Gītā* to be a song sung by the Brāhmaṇas chiefly for the benefit of the Kṣatriya and Brāhmaṇa classes. Thus, he finds the *Gītā*'s devotionalism or *bhakti* to serve well in stabilizing a feudal society and maintaining the Brāhmaṇas as 'a superstitious leisure class'.[30] When the song addresses itself to the socially disadvantaged, it still, in Kosambi's opinion, speaks exclusively from a Brāhmaṇical perspective:[31]

> We hear from the mouth of Kṛṣṇa himself (G. 9.32): 'For those who take refuge in Me, be they even of the sinful breeds such as women, vaiśyas, and śūdras . . .' That is, all women and all men of the working and producing classes are defiled by their very birth, though they may in [the] after-life be freed by their faith in the god who degrades them so casually in this one. Not only that, the god himself had created such differences (G. 4.13): 'The four-caste (-class) division has been created by Me'; this is proclaimed in the list of great achievements.

There is little doubt then that Kosambi finds little in the realm of social ethics as promulgated in the *Gītā* to be worth saving in the modern world: 'There is no need to dig into the *Gītā* or the Bible for an ethical system sandwiched with pure superstition. Such books can still be enjoyed for their aesthetic value. Those who claim more usually try to shackle the minds of other people, and to impede man's progress, under the most specious claims.'[32]

In his introduction to the *Subhāṣitaratnakoṣa*,[33] Kosambi shows an equal willingness to assail the poetry collected in the anthologies and, beyond that, Sanskrit poetry in general. As with the *Gītā*, he is willing to concede a qualified aesthetic approval to this literature, but gives the tenor of his objections to it when he declares 'The poetry which we find in our *subhāṣitas* necessarily carries with the rank beauty of an orchid the corresponding atmosphere of luxury, parasitism, decay.'[34] He develops, then, the notion that Sanskrit poetry was first and last a product of a talented though decadent *class*, divorced from the realities of everyday life as lived by the common man to a degree such that it would have been not just *unwilling* but also *unable* to speak of human experience except as idealized in the court or in the monastery.

By focusing on 'court and monastery', Kosambi means not only to designate the Brāhmaṇas and the ruling Kṣatriyas, but to underscore their alliance in isolation from the rest of their society. Both groups, he asserts, enjoyed 'some sort of guaranteed living'.[35] By virtue of its mystique of refinement and sacerdotalism, Sanskrit itself was to take on a market value in this patrician alliance. The Brāhmaṇa class itself was 'responsible for keeping both ritual and language alive while regarding itself as superior to the rest of the people'; but, 'this could not have succeeded without a working alliance with the ruling class, for which again there is ample testimony.'[36] For their part, the ruling Kṣatriyas found in the mastery—or, at least, in the patronage—of Sanskrit a means of social advancement and the legitimatization of their rule. Kosambi cites the example of Harṣa here. If the ruler would lead the way, it would be inevitable then that the court would follow, thus further solidifying Sanskrit's position as the superior language. Thus, 'with its claim to immemorial antiquity [it] become a sort of court language for records, and intercourse between regions that had developed their own languages.'[37] Thus was a market created for Sanskrit poets and their verse.

But the artificiality of the social alliance which gave rise to this market was to impose corresponding limitations upon the robust and independent growth of the literature it nurtured. The poet himself, Kosambi argues, was supremely conscious of the fact that he was addressing not the whole of his society but an isolated faction at its crest. Therefore, he was ill-disposed to bite the hand that feeds: 'If the Sanskrit poet had been conscious of his failings, which were those of his society, there would at least have been powerful satire, of which no example is to be seen except perhaps ridiculous exaggeration.'[38] For, he 'could not attack the foundation of his own being, for he was attached to society by the slender thread which dangled him from a particular decadent class.'[39] If the poets took notice of poverty, nature and the experiences of travel, they were still mainly writing for the court and the monastery; so the overwhelming majority of their compositions were on the themes of sex and religion, varied with outrageous exercises in courtly flattery. The poet was, then, 'a talking house-bird'[40] singing the luxurious life of the privileged few. But even his religious outpourings had their uses: the class structure could well exploit the belief in common gods and the inevitability of caste to retain its dominance without recourse to material force.[41]

With its poets so compromised, it is small wonder, Kosambi concludes, that the resultant literature is as thoroughly unreliable in depicting 'any Indian's character or thought. . .as the Mughal-Rajput paintings of Pṛthvī-rāja, dressed in Mughal style, and sporting luxuriant mustaches on a progressively fatter face with fatter body.'[42]

Dev Raj Chanana

In an article entitled 'The Sanskritist and Indian Society'[43] Dev Raj Chanana attacks the question of the achievement of Sanskrit literature from an interesting new angle. He begins by noting that hopes were raised in India for a revival of the Sanskrit heritage after the achievement of independence. Publishing increased and numerous new academic commissions and teaching positions were created. With all this the Sanskritist in India might well have expected the popular estimation of his worth to the nation to take a dramatic rise. Chanana notes that this has not been so: the disconsolate Indian Sanskritist remains as much as ever 'the butt of ridicule, . . .an "animal without horns and tail".'[44] Chanana finds the popular explanation of this phenomenon—that India suffers from an all-inclusive craze for Westernization—to be superficial, and he invites us instead to take a look at the activities of Indian Sanskritists in the recent past.

Although Chanana promises a treatment of the 'recent activities' of the Sanskritists, what he gives us instead is a comprehensive and often amusing catalogue of Hindu toadyism and sycophancy from as far back as the Muslim invasions. What made the Muslim invaders unique was their marked success in resisting the assimilation of the Hindu ideology which had engulfed so many previous invaders. For the first time, the Sanskritists found *their* ideology threatened, and the same ideology *required* them to resist. Inscriptional evidence points instead to the fact that the Sanskritists exhausted the *kāvya* repertoire of hyperbolic praise in the flattery of their conquerors; and most vexing to Chanana, at the same time they turned away from any perception of the woes of the common people. Chanana cites a number of examples how even the Hindu gods and goddesses were employed in the service of the heretical conquerors. The following is but one example:[45]

> In the words of its author, Udayarāja, Mahmood Shah, a thorough-going Muslim, was 'the protector of Hindu Dharma', as if he were an orthodox Hindu being. Describing him as a kṣatriya king, the poet writes that he is served by both Sarasvatī and Śrī, that he is more liberal than even Karṇa and that his ancestor, Muzaffar Khan had helped Śrī Kṛṣṇa against Kali-Kāla.

This kind of wholesale sell-out to the conqueror on the Sanskritist's part was in contrast to the more candid expressions which the poets of the Bhakti movement voiced in the vernaculars: 'Nanak, for example, moved by the sufferings of the common peoples, had exclaimed, "Here comes Babur, at the head of the marriage-procession of Sin".'[46] Urdu poets sang of the common people of both religions. Chanana finds the silence of the Sanskritist on the subject of his people's misery a failure to provide the ideological leadership his society had a right to expect. Instead, we find the Brāhmaṇas of Madhyadeśa recognizing Akbar, who consolidated Mughal power during his reign, as 'the highest, the purest among all the Brahmins!'[47] Of all the Sanskritists who served in Mughal courts, perhaps the only one to retain a measure of his integrity was the celebrated Jagannātha Paṇḍita-rāja who had the candour to write as follows: 'I beg not [from] the petty Hindu, who donates a copper-vessel on an auspicious day. I beg from the great Mughal for whom a canopy of gold is but straw."[48]

Still better was

> One of the rare instances of social criticism [which] occurs in

> a verse of the *Abdulla-caritam* of Lakṣmīdhara (ed. by J. B. Chaudhuri, Calcutta, 1947), where the poet warns against trusting the kings and gives as proof the fact that Aurangzeb had imprisoned his own father, Shajehan (v. 10 and 11).[49]

Chanana adds, 'It is interesting that whatever little was written by way of social protest, direct or veiled, has to be dated before A.D. 1,000. We have in mind the *Mṛcchakaṭikam* and the *śatakas* of Bhartṛhari.''[50]

Instead, collaboration of a notably obsequious variety replaced social protest throughout the British era. Some eighty Banaras *paṇḍitas* dispatched to England a testimonial to the 'generous and enlightened policy of the illustrious, noble Mr. Hastings, the Governor-General'[51]—that for the notorious Hastings! The leader of the Vaiṣṇava sect of Surat, the Gosvāminī Mahārājñī, addressed Lord Cornwallis as one 'the sun-like splendour of whose terrible and firmly consolidated power is scorching the faces of his *enemy's* wives.'[52] The Gosvāminī did not specify whether she meant by 'enemy's wives' those of Indians in general or more particularly those of the hundreds of thousands of poor cultivators deprived of their ancestral land and plunged even deeper into poverty by Cornwallis' fiat.[53] The *paṇḍitas* of Puri wrote that Lord Wellesley—a *mleccha* after all—was responsible for the protection of *their* gods, the Brāhmaṇas and the Vaiṣṇavas.[54] The same group notes that they 'are praying night and day to God that the supremacy of the English power may last forever. . . .'[55] A later Sanskritist was to write on the occasion of the coronation of George V that 'Śrī and Viṣṇu have come to the earth in the forms of Mary and George for our protection.'[56]

If this servility to the British were matched by an equal humility toward their own people, Chanana might well have found it easier to forgive the *paṇḍitas* who produced these cringing documents on such a prolific scale. Instead he finds an attitude among them that their society should serve *them*, even though they formed the vanguard of those opposing every progressive reform designed to benefit the disadvantaged among their own people. We have already noted the apathy displayed by the Sanskrit *paṇḍitas* with regard to the suffering of their fellows; it would also be appropriate to consider the words of the celebrated Śivājī, whose opposition to Aurangzeb is sung even today in a number of contemporary Sanskrit *mahākāvyas*. Chanana notes that Śivājī is reputed to have declared on the subject of the 'common people' that 'Money is inconvenient for them: give them Victuals and an Arse-Clout, it is enough.'[57] Apart from glorifying a hero of this stamp, the *paṇḍitas* continued to display haughtiness to their fellows, fondly repeating, '*brahma-vākyaṃ Janārdanaḥ*', that a Brāhmaṇa's word is that of God himself, 'without', as Chanana says, 'ever bothering about the consequences of his "fiats" given out in the name of holy scriptures.'[58] On this point, Chanana cites Rabindranath Tagore, who wrote: 'In those times, the Brahmin was called *bhūdeva*, god on earth; this godhead does not carry the inescapable greatness; it merely claims without any rhyme or reason, his superiority [over others]. This superiority without reason was above right or wrong.'[59] It is not surprising then to find the Brāhmaṇas 'excommunicating' their countrymen for the sin of travelling overseas; defending the practice of widow-immolation on the basis of a single corrupt reading of the *Ṛgveda*; opposing the abolition of slavery in India; or, denigrating a reform-minded one of their own, Ishwarachandra Vidyasagar, who dared to plead for the sanction of widow-remarriage.[60]

In the light of such an undeniable failure of leadership on the part of the Sanskrit *paṇḍitas* of his own land, Chanana not surprisingly is moved to question the very value of Sanskrit learning at any time, but especially in today's world. He quotes Rammohan Roy with obvious approval: ' "The Sanskrit system of education would be the best calculated to keep this country in darkness"....and that "the pupils will here acquire what was known two thousand years ago, with the addition of vain and empty subtleties" '.[61] Chanana feels that the failure of Sanskrit education can be traced at least as far back as the eleventh century A.D. He cites Al-Biruni's amazement that the Indians, who at one time welcomed learning from the Greeks, should have so recently become' "haughty, foolishly vain, self-conceited and stolid. They are niggardly in communicating that which they know and they take the greatest care to withhold it from men of another caste, among their own people. . . ." [62]

> Now-a-days [Chanana concludes], the only section of [the] intelligentsia to whom this description still applies is that of the Sanskritist. He is unaware of the simple fact that his knowledge is centuries-old and needs to be revivified. Refusing to learn this basic fact, he keeps on satiating his thirst at this ancestral well, whose water, having turned brackish about a thousand years ago, is now putrid, rancid. Having cut himself off from the advance of modern India, he suffers from an acute form of inferiority-complex and alternates between conformism and chauvinism. Little realizing the ludicrous nature of his efforts, he is subject to fits of sulking and sullenness. Obviously the remedy lies first and foremost in his realizing the nature of this, his malady. Only this realization coupled with efforts at comprehending the modern reality will help him. Till this is begun and achieved. the Sanskritist is doomed to a life of vegetation.[63]

Sanskrit Studies

With Dev Raj Chanana's challenge still before us, we have now come full circle and confront again the problem of justifying Sanskrit studies. It would be useless to deny that the outlook would be a very gloomy one indeed *if* the achievement of Sanskrit literature and the benefit derived from its study were in fact as severely limited as our critics have argued. For who would care to defend artificialities spun out expressly for an audience of literary fops? (And, in so doing, be counted among them!) Who would inflict upon a busy world the reading of the Brāhmaṇas' obsequious *praśastis* and their own *ātmastutis*? Who would wish to declare before his colleagues that he has prepared the last decade for a professional career devoted to the pursuit of vain and empty subtleties? And, in fact, it *would* be difficult to differ sharply with A. B. Keith, S. N. Dasgupta, and S. K. De over their assessments of the most celebrated literary monuments in Sanskrit. There can be no doubt that within this range these critics have read their texts and read them well; any additional criticism which I might offer would be a matter of emphasis rather than of substance. But apart from these, the most heavily trodden pathways of the literature, I find my judgement increasingly going its own way. For it is there in the more remote, even wilder, regions of the literature—in the satires and farces, and in the vast areas of *kathā* and *subhāṣita* literature—where I believe anyone who wishes to defend the integrity of any part of Sanskrit literature must make his stand. From these vantage points it will be possible to point to the copious satirizing of false ascetics and nuns together with vainglorious and hypocritical Brāhmaṇas: this in reply to the charge that Sanskrit was only used to bolster 'the monastery'. From here, the sycophantic praise of a nation's rules may be balanced against the sharp complaints of those who served those rulers. From here the *bhakti* so well exploited by the ruling classes will be countered with tales which warn of the exploitation of the superstitious by the clever and the amoral. After exploring these regions, it will be easier to assess the truth in the charges that Sanskrit can offer no echo of social discontent, nothing by way of social protest after A.D. 1000 no powerful satire.

Moreover, this area of Sanskrit literature, when re-examined, will, I believe, put to rest the notion that its creators and their audience were necessarily devoid of social conscience. Even D. D. Kosambi admits that the poets take note of poverty. Selections from this literature will show that regard of poverty to be neither all that rare nor unsympathetic. If the Sanskrit poets are accused of singing the joys of the unexamined life, our selections will contain the suggestion that ignorance is far from bliss. If their poetry is attacked for its recondite artificiality, we shall see them burlesque vain and empty pedantry. If they are styled the 'talking house-birds' of their rulers, we shall see them rail against the prostitution of their art. And, D. D. Kosambi notwithstanding, it seems to me that the image of the Sanskrit poet which emerges from the *subhāṣita-saṅgrahas* reveals a good deal more than the genteel lackey so often suggested. The verses to be examined will show their authors working in a milieu not suffused with the languor of the dilettante, but alive with captious, even vicious, critics; with rivals disposed to marketing plagarism, pedantry, sycophancy and bombast—these poets spoke out against these very failings in Sanskrit poetry long ago. In sum, this literature will provide us with a much sharper perspective on both the Sanskrit poet *and* his society, undeniably more reliable than Kosambi's Mughal-Rajput paintings.

All of this, hopefully, might prove useful for the revivification of Sanskrit studies. Reformers like Kosambi and Chanana may now look back to find the antecedents of their criticisms of the literature within the literature itself. It may be admitted that the overwhelming preponderance of material considered here falls outside the normal curriculum of Sanskrit instruction as it is conducted today; perhaps those wishing to foster social conscience among those intellectuals traditional-minded enough to embark upon Sanskrit study would do well to introduce this kind of material into their curricula. It is difficult to believe that all students are so alike that a few might not enjoy and learn more from Kṣemendra's satire of bureaucrats than from the mawkish sentimentality of the *Abhijñānaśākuntalam*.

The Purpose and Procedure of the Study

As already indicated, the purpose of this study is to re-examine Sanskrit literature as it relates to its society in the light of evidence drawn from a variety of sources, but primarily from the satires, farces, *kathā* and *subhāṣita* literatures. If it can be shown that significant manifestations of social conscience do exist in these sources, then the type of assessments of the achievement of Sanskrit literature cited above would be shown to stand in need of amendment.

It seems obvious that the primary responsibility of such a study should be the presentation of passages reflecting social conscience; such a procedure will be followed here. In addition, the passages adduced in evidence will be accompanied by analysis assessing their relevance to the types of criticism considered above.

Scope of the Study

In addition to satires, farces, *kathās* and *subhāṣitas*, reference will also be made to at least one history, Kalhaṇa's *Rājataraṅgiṇī*. As it is a part of my purpose to show that reflections of social conscience are hardly unknown even in the classics, passages will be cited from the *Daśakumāracarita*, the *śatakas* of Bhartṛhari, the animal fables of the *Pañcatantra* and *Hitopadeśa*, Bāṇa's *Kādambarī*, and the *Mṛcchakaṭika*. If the sources are many, the material in them which could be utilized seems endless. Consequently, no attempt will be made here to reproduce *every* passage which suits our purpose; instead, the aim will be to show the following: first of all, that such material *exists* in abundance; second of all, where it may be found; and, third of all, its main characteristics. Even in a study of this length it will be impossible to present anything comprehensive of the relevant material in the satires of Kṣemendra *alone*,[64] much less that in all the *bhāṇas*, *prahasanas* and *subhāṣita-saṅgrahas*. This study seeks merely to break the ground.

Limitations

Just as every *verse* of social criticism cannot be included here, even so I thought it advisable not to attempt to include even every *type* of social criticism to be found in the literature under consideration. For example, though a rather sizeable body of literature exists condemning the wiles of prostitutes,[65] I felt its inclusion would be tangential to any reply to the criticisms cited above. Similarly, criticisms directed at the consumption of alcohol and tobacco have also been ruled out. Although a great many verses critical of the wealthy have been considered, those included in this study usually possess some other element, such as an injunction to one's fellow poets not to grovel before the rich. In the area of social criticism I have thought it most germane to limit consideration mainly to the alliance Kosambi has designated 'the monastery and the court', and have included numerous verses critical of the religious and the politically powerful: the hypocrisy of Brāhmaṇas; the venality of monks and nuns; the stupidity of kings, the perfidy of their counsellors, the petty rivalry of their courtiers, and the corruption of their bureaucrats. If references voicing these criticisms seem numerous and somewhat repetitive, it is hoped that their relevance to a response to the charge that 'no social protest exists in Sanskrit' will be seen as justification for their inclusion.

References

1. F. Max-Müller, *A History of Ancient Sanskrit Literature*, p. 73.
2. Ibid.
3. Ibid., pp. 42-43.
4. Ibid., p. 45.
5. *Aitareya-Brāhmaṇa*, II.19, as translated by A.B. Keith in his *Ṛg-Veda Brāhmaṇas Translated*, p. 148.
6. Müller, op. cit., pp. 51-53.
7. A.B. Keith, *The Sanskrit Drama*. (Hereafter SD) p. 276.
8. Ibid., pp. 276-79.

9. Ibid., pp. 278-83.

10. Ibid., pp. 276-83 passim.

11. Keith, *SD*, pp. 285-86. Keith here alludes to the plot of Kālidāsa's *Mālavikāgnimitram*. Perhaps an even better example of the restrictions imposed upon romantic love by the Brāhmaṇas' rigid, hierarchical structuring of society might be found in Kālidāsa's *Abhijñānaśākuntalam* (A-S). There the royal hero encounters the heroine in the role of a hermit-child and fears that the might well be a Brāhmaṇī, out of his class and therefore ineligible for marriage. Kālidāsa allows his hero to resolve his doubts in a verse embodying a memorable example of Hindu reasoning: "Doubtless, she *is* suitable for marriage to a Kṣatriya, as my noble mind lusts for her." *A-S*, I.19 (NSP ed.). The one well-known play which transcended the stultifying conventions outlined above was, as Keith duly notes at several places, the *Mṛcchakaṭikam*. Still the name traditionally given to the author—Śūdraka—makes one doubt that the author could have been a Brāhmaṇa. Keith dismisses the notion that the author was a famous king on pp. 128-30 of his *SD*.

12. Keith, *HSL*, p. 345. Barbra Stoler Miller cites the same passage in her *Bhartṛhari: Poems* (p. xviii) and declares, 'But even if we found that every other Sanskrit poet conformed to the stereotype, Bhartṛhari would defy the mold.' As we shall see, scores of other poets shared this non-conformity with Bhartṛihari.

13. *HSLCP*, Preface, p. xi.

14. Ibid., pp. xiv-xvi of the Introduction.

15. Ibid., p. xvi.

16. Ibid., pp. xxii-xl.

17. Ibid., p. xciii.

18. Ibid., pp. xxvii-xxviii.

19. Ibid., p. 19.

20. Ibid.

21. Keith, *SD*, pp. 284-85; *HSL*, pp. 29ff.

22. Dasgupta, *HSLCP*, pp. lv-lvi.

23. Keith, *SD*, p. 285.

24. De, *HSLCP*, p. 36.

25. Ibid., p. 37.

26. Bombay, Popular Prakashan, 1962. The essay is called 'Social and Economic Aspects of the *Bhagavad-Gītā*' and is found on pp. 12-41.

27. Ibid., p. 17.

28. Ibid.

29. Ibid., p. 12.

30. Ibid., pp. 29-33.

31. Ibid., p. 15.

32. Ibid., p. 37.

33. D.D. Kosambi and V.V. Gokhale, Ed., *HOS* vol. 42, 1957.

34. Ibid., p. xliv.

35. Ibid., p. xlviii.

36. Ibid.,

37. Ibid., p. xlix.

38. Ibid., p. lx.

39. Ibid.
40. Ibid., p. xlvii.
41. Ibid., p. lviii.
42. Ibid., p. l.
43. Published in the Indian Journal, *Enquiry*, New Series, vol. II, no. 2—(Old Series no. 11)—dated Monsoon 1965.
44. Ibid., p. 50.
45. Ibid., p. 52, citing H.D. Sankalia, 'Dohad Inscription of Mahmood Begra' *Ep. Ind.*, pp. 1-2, Sanskrit verses, Canto II, vv. 1-2.
46. Ibid., p. 53.
47. Ibid., p. 54.
48. Ibid., p. 55, citing the epilogue of the *Āsafa-vilāsa*, *Paṇḍita-rāja-kāvya-saṅgraha*, Hyderabad, 1958, p. 85.
49. Ibid., p. 57, fn. 42.
50. Ibid.
51. Ibid., p. 58, citing S.N. Sen and Umesh Mishra, *Sanskrit Documents*, Allahabad, 1951, pp. 66ff.
52. Ibid., p. 59, citing the same source, p. 80ff. The underscoring is Chanana's.
53. Ibid., p. 59.
54. Ibid., citing the same source, p. 90ff.
55. Ibid., citing the same source, p. 91.
56. Ibid., p. 62, citing the *Makuṭa-bandha*, Madras, 1912, the last verse.
57. Ibid., p. 57, citing a reference in Irfan Habib, *The Agrarian System of Mughal India*, Bombay, 1963, n. 2, p. 90.
58. Ibid., p. 61.
59. Ibid., p. 60, citing 'Kālāntara', *Rabīndra Racanāvalī*, Calcutta, vol. 13, p. 211.
60. Ibid., pp. 61-63. Apropos of the corrupt text used to sanction *satī*, Chanana remarks that 'the cries of hundreds of widows, often tied to the pyre, could not move the Sanskritist at least to verify the genuineness of the stanza in question.' (n. 60, pp. 62-63).
61. Ibid., p. 64, citing the *Advanced History of India*, London, 1950, p. 817.
62. Ibid., p. 66, citing *Al-Biruni's India*, translated by Sachau, London, 1888, vol. I, pp. 22-23.
63. Ibid., pp. 66-67.
64. This writer has already begun work on what he hopes will be full-length studies of this sort of material in Kṣemendra's satires and the *subhāṣita-saṅgrahas*.
65. E.g., Dāmodaragupta's *Kuṭṭanī-mata;* Kṣemendra's *Samayaemātṛkā*, and the fourth chapter of his *Kalā-vilāsa*. Cf. Ludwik Strenbach, *Gaṇikā-vṛtta-saṅgraha*, Vishveshvaranand Indological Series, no. 4. Hoshiarpur, 1953.

Chapter 1

THE ORIGINS OF A SECULAR LITERATURE IN SANSKRIT

Legendary Accounts

Exact knowledge of the origins of a secular literature in Sanskrit remains quite beyond our grasp. The Indian traditions on this subject are viewed today as legend rather than fact. Vālmīki has been traditionally honoured with being the first poet or *ādi-kavi*. The *Rāmāyaṇa* ascribed to him relates that the basic metrical form of Sanskrit poetry, the *śloka* stanza, was born spontaneously of Vālmīki's grief upon seeing a bird slain by a hunter. The story says further that the god Brahmā appeared at Vālmīki's hermitage and commanded the sage to commit to verse the story of Rāma. And just as the *Rāmāyaṇa* provides traditions concerning its legendary composer, Vālmīki, the *Mahābhārata* likewise relates tales of incidents in the life of its legendary composer, Vyāsa. Traditions from the *Mahābhārata* and elsewhere credit Vyāsa with performing the literary equivalent of the labours of Hercules: the editing of the Vedas for transmission to the present era, and the composition of eighteen major and eighteen minor *Purāṇas*, as well as the *Vyāsasmṛti*, the *Vedānta-Sūtra*, and a commentary on the *Yoga-Sūtras* of Patañjali. These stories have an undeniable charm, but they are not held to represent historical fact beyond the frontiers of India today.

Modern Speculations

Although they lack the narrative charm of the Indian legends, many of the early speculations of literary historians in the West have also come into question. One such notion was propounded by M. Winternitz, who speculated that the epics owed their composition to the *sūtas*, a class of men who were both bards and charioteers. As charioteers, the *sūtas* would have been the witnesses of much which occurred in battle; off the battlefields, they would have recounted their patron's heroic deeds and also would have embellished their narratives with accounts of the circumstances of courtly life which surrounded these events. Winternitz also found in the inferior social rank of the *sūtas* a convenient explanation for the simple style and non-Pāṇinian grammatical irregularities of the epics. He argued that the *sūtas*, as low-caste offspring of non-sanctioned (*pratiloma*) marriages of Kṣatriya males with socially superior Brāhmaṇa females, might well have been denied access to the type of Sanskrit employed by the Brāhmaṇas in the correct performance of their sacrificial rites. Moreover, the *Vāyu Purāṇa* informs us that the *sūtas* were 'used to preserve the pedigrees of kings and great men and also the traditions of learning and books.'[1]

Although Winternitz's *sūta*-theory does seem to offer an attractive explanation of the origin and stylistic peculiarities of the epics, Surendranath Dasgupta declares that there is really little evidence to support it. Surveying the literature, Dasgupta found no references to the *sūtas* as the singers of the successes of kings and lesser heroes in battle. He did find, however, that the *sūtas* were employed in the much more mundane tasks of tending horses and elephants, cooking their kings' food, and, of course, driving chariots.[2]

Dasgupta himself suggests that one might better regard the poetry of both the epic and classical periods as direct development from the literature of the Vedic period or at least from the time of the composition of the early Upaniṣads. At least this is what his text seems to suggest. His exact statement is: 'Though it is needless to trace the origin of Sanskrit Kāvyas to the Vedas or the Brāhmaṇas, it cannot be decided [presumably a misprint for 'denied'] that some of the early Upaniṣads like the *Kaṭha*, *Muṇḍaka* and the *Śvetāśvatara* contain verses in the classical style. Indeed the style of the *Mahābhārata* and the *Gītā* may be regarded as the prolongation of the classical style which had already begun at the time of the Upaniṣads'; and his marginal notice reads 'Direct evolution of the classical style from the Vedic literature.'[3] He goes on to bolster his argument for a continuity by noting that 'Rhetoricians in a much later time have quoted verses from the *Mahābhārata* to demonstrate the theory of *vyañjanā* and *guṇībhūta-vyañjanā*',[4] and declaring that 'the atmosphere of the *Rāmāyaṇa* is not far removed from that of Kālidāsa.'[5]

However, to my mind it is difficult to see how Dasgupta's evidence compels belief in a direct evolution of the classical style from that of the Vedic literature. To begin with, it seems that Dasgupta makes too much of *upamā* ('well-known even in Vedic times'[6]), *vyañjanā*, and *guṇībhūta-vyañjanā*. How the three terms merely refer to simile, poetic suggestion, and situations in which the suggested sense is more striking than the declared import, respectively, and it is difficult to imagine that most of the world's literature from all times does not exhibit these commonplace elements. I find his observation that 'the atmosphere of the *Rāmāyaṇa* is not far removed from that of Kālidāsa' to be similarly unconvincing. In the first place, I am not entirely sure that the observation is correct. To be sure, there are elements of the supernatural in Kālidāsa's works: there are, for instance, romances depicted between divine personages (Śiva and Pārvatī in the *Kumārasaṃbhava*), between demi-gods (the *yakṣa* and *yakṣī* in the *Meghadūta*), and between a celestial nymph and an earthly king (Urvaśī and Pururavas in the *Vikramorvaśīya*); yet these and even such elements as Raghu's battle with Indra and Duṣyanta's airborne chariot appear to me to be rather mundane when contrasted with the following fantastic elements in the *Rāmāyaṇa*: a doe-born sage with a horn on his forehead who reaches manhood unaware of the female sex (Ṛṣyaśṛṅga); demons with three or even ten heads (Khara or Rāvaṇa); a giant monkey who bounds across 800 miles of ocean; or a defeat of the demonic forces at the hands of a contingent of monkeys and bears. Yet even if we concede that Kālidāsa and the *Rāmāyaṇa* call for equal efforts of the will to suspend disbelief, it still does not seem to me that incidents involving divine or semi-divine characters or superhuman feats or even animals with human characteristics are so rare in ancient literature that their presence in two places could be thought to establish continuity, much less a 'direct evolution'.

The Case for a pre-Aśvaghoṣan Kāvya Literature

Although there may well have been a fully-developed *kāvya* literature before Aśvaghoṣa's time, a fair amount of the evidence which had been adduced to support this conclusion now appears less convincing than it did when A.B. Keith wrote his *History of Sanskrit Literature*.

The primary difficulty of course is that nothing of a pre-Aśvaghoṣan *kāvya* literature has been recovered; literary historians have consequently been forced to fall back on references to such *kāvya* to be found in works thought to antedate Aśvaghoṣa. The most important of these sources has been thought to be the *Mahābhāṣya* of Patañjali, written to explain the *Aṣṭādhyāyī* of Pāṇini. Before considering the case that can be made from the Patañjali references, it should be noted that some speculations concerning early *kāvya* have centred upon Pāṇini himself. Pāṇini distinguished between the Vedic language, which he termed *chandas*, and another type of language which he termed *bhāṣā*. It has been speculated that the latter type may have been drawn from a well-developed popular literature of a secular character extant in Pāṇini's time and earlier. There is also a popular tradition that Pāṇini himself was a poet: from the eleventh century A.D. and later have come references to Pāṇini as a distinguished composer of verses in the Upajāti metre and as the author of a *mahākāvya*, *Jāmbavatī-Vijaya* and another *Pātāla-Vijaya*, which may have been only another name for the first work. The problem with these references is that they are very late—fully a millennium-and-a-half after Pāṇini's estimated era—and we do not know today whether these few, brief references from a much later time were based upon reliable evidence then available, or were simply passing on a mistaken tradition.

Returning to Patañjali, we find that he mentions a *Vāraruca Kāvya*[7] and names three *ākhyāyikās*, but describes them no further. He also remarks upon the practice of taking poetic licence, saying *chandovat kavayaḥ kurvanti.*[8] But the one aspect of Patañjali's *Mahābhāṣya* which has proved the most intriguing to literary historians, A.B. Keith and S.K. De, is some forty citations which, though ofted fragmentary, betray an unmistakable *kāvya* treatment of lyric, epic, panegyric and gnomic themes. Moreover, many of the quotations are presented in metres not to be found in the Vedic literature but *are* widely employed in the later *kāvya* of the classical era. Such metres as the Indravajrā, the Upajāti, the Śālinī and the Vaṃśastha all occur in grammatical verses called *kārikās*, many of which antedate the *Mahābhāṣya*. *Kārikās* are verses intended for memorization. These elegant new metres must have almost certainly originated in a secular *kāvya* literature of the time, because simpler prosodic forms would have been more practical for teaching grammar.[9] Thus, it would seem that the *Mahābhāṣya* offers convincing evidence for the existence of a *kāvya* literature before Aśvaghoṣa's period.

Yet the whole argument from the *Mahābhāṣya* in so far as it bears upon a pre-Aśvaghoṣan *kāvya* literature hangs on the traditionally accepted date of the second century B.C. for Patañjali; and this date has been challenged since 1930. This fact came to my attention recently when reading a review of J.F. Staal's *A Reader on the Sanskrit Grammarians.* It includes an essay by R.G. Bhandarkar in which the author advanced arguments leading to the conclusion that Patañjali's comment on Pāṇini's *sūtra* 3.2.123 was written between 144 B.C. and 142 B.C. In his introduction to the article, Staal notes that Frauwallner has suggested a more recent date in a study published in 1960.[10] The author of the review,. J.W. de Jong, notes further that 'Louis de La Vallee Poussin had already in 1930 given sound arguments for a later date [than the second century B.C.].'[11]

A similar uncertainty now attaches itself to Piṅgala's *Chandaḥsūtra.* As the book has come down to us, it is mainly concerned with the analysis of metrical forms drawn from non-Vedic sources. Given the reputed antiquity of the text, A.B. Keith declared that the *sūtras* 'suggest a period of transition in which the authors of the erotic lyric were trying experiment after experiment in metrical effect'; this, be it remembered, as long ago as the sixth century B.C. But, as with the *Mahābhāṣya*, more recent critics have questioned the date of the *Chandaḥsūtra*, or at least the portion dealing with non-Vedic metres. M. Ghosh holds that the two sections of the work are by quite different authors.[12] Another scholar, D.C. Sircar, argues that the part dealing with classical metres cannot be dated earlier than the fifth century A.D.[13]

Before moving on to Aśvaghoṣa, we should take note of speculations concerning supposed secular currents within the Vedic literature itself. Max-Müller was one of the early scholars to believe that he had discerned another, less hieratical inspiration in some hymns than that which gave rise to those of a purely religious sort which dominate the *Ṛgveda.* He draws our attention to the 103rd hymn of the 7th Maṇḍala, attributed to the *ṛṣi*, Vasiṣṭha. In this hymn, according to Müller's reading of it, the chanting of the Brāhmaṇas at the Soma rite and the mechanical repetition of hymns by Brāhmaṇa students rehearsing their lessons are compared humorously to the croaking of frogs. Müller declares the hymn to be 'clearly a satire on the priests; and it is curious to observe that the same animal should have been chosen by the Vedic satirist to represent the priests, which by the earliest satirist of Greece was selected as the representative of the Homeric heroes.'[14] Müller felt that this hymn belonged to 'an imitative, reflecting, and criticizing age', and that 'there seems thus to be little room for doubt, if we consider the character of this and similar hymns, that we must make a distinction between two periods in the history of Vedic poetry, the one primitive, the other secondary.'[15]

But Müller's interpretation of the frog hymn, while convincing some, has by now been met with a chorus of disagreement. In an article with the strongly-worded title 'The So-Called Secular, Humorous and Satirical Hymns of the Ṛgveda', J. Gonda notes that M. Haug had realized that the comparison was meant to be serious, the comparison with the Brāhmaṇa's intended to underscore the sacred character of the frogs' utterances.[16] Frogs were thought to bring on precious rain, as were the Brāhmaṇas with their Soma rites. Considering the importance which rainfall holds to any agrarian society, Gonda and others—rightly, in my opinion—conclude that the analogies are no joking matter; in fact, 'these similes in the frog-hymn may [themselves] be considered as having a magical effect, as containing power.'[17]

Passing beyond the frog-hymn, Gonda systematically analyzes a number of other allegedly secular hymns of the *Ṛgveda*, often pointing to parallel occurrences in the *Atharvaveda*, concluding in each of these cases that the verses in question in all likelihood had serious, significance in the minds of the Vedic poets and their audience.

All this would suggest that the *Ṛgveda* holds very little if anything of a secular tradition enfolded among its ritual prayers. Yet, other scholars have pointed to verses of a cynical, gnomic variety, speculating that these verses might be drawn from secular sources. Several of these gnomic observations denigrate womankind. Thus the *Śatapatha Brāhmaṇa* relegates women to the rank of the Śūdra, the dog and the crow; while the *Maitrāyaṇī Saṃhitā* equates them with dice and drink in terms of evil.[18] In a similar vein, the *Aitareya Brāhmaṇa* contrasts the blessing of a son's birth with the curse of that of a daughter:

> A wife is a comrade, a daughter a misery,
> And a son a light in the highest heaven.[19]

Terming these thoughts 'witty, but cynical', S.K. De goes on to declare that

> These and other secular hymns, some of which are of a narrative character, as well as short legends in the Brāhmaṇas, are indications that contemporaneous with the religious literature of the Veda, there probably existed a profane literature which is now lost, but from which in course of time emerged, on the one hand, the rich collection of tales and fables in the Buddhist and Jaina literature, and on the other, the narrative miscellany of the Epic and Purāṇa literature, with their diversified content of inexhaustible legendary and didactic material.[20]

I would agree that the type of gnomic verses quoted above are 'cynical', if not 'witty'; at the same time, I doubt very much that their authors would have regarded them as either. Whether or not passages in the *Brāhmaṇas* distinctive for narrative qualities or the recounting of legends do indeed constitute 'indications' that 'there probably existed a profane literature which is now lost' seems unclear; in my judgement, it would seem equally plausible that these passages grew to meet the need for providing a rationale for parts of the ritual the basis of which had become obscure by the time of the composition of the *Brāhmaṇas.* Moreover, we have already seen that Gonda's article should give one pause before presupposing, as De does, 'these and other *secular* hymns' [my underscoring]. Gonda, for his part, is reluctant to concede a secular origin for hymns of the *Ṛgveda,* even for obscure hymns of the 10th Maṇḍala. He concludes that 'it is not only possible, but even highly probable that in a part of the 10th book and in a certain number of hymns of the other books we possess remainders of the religious literature of other circles and groups of ancient Indian society than those Brāhmaṇical priest-families who concentrated on their own hieratic matter and their own rites.'[21]

By way of summarizing this whole search for secular literature antecedent to Aśvaghoṣa's surprisingly sophisticated *kāvyas*, we must note in the beginning that a number of what seemed promising lines of research have proved to be chimerical. For now it would seem acceptable to follow tradition and turn to the *Rāmāyaṇa* for the earliest *kāvya.* Nor should we overlook the *Mahābhārata*, though it lacks the polish of the *Rāmāyaṇa* and has been traditionally classed as an *Itihāsa.*

Buddhist Voices

It will come as no surprise that some of the most cutting criticism of Brāhmaṇism should come from Buddhist and Jaina sources. Yet I believe that these partisan criticisms should not be ignored for several reasons. To begin with, although a parallel or two is noted in the Pali literature, the critical literature considered below is in Sanskrit, the Brāhmaṇas' stock in trade. Obviously then, not all of Sanskrit literature was concerned with the Brāhmaṇas' self-glorification. Here in Buddhist literature, Sanskrit is used to upset the pre-eminence of its traditional custodians. Next, I believe it important to review these Buddhist criticisms of Brāhmaṇism in order to facilitate comparison with Hindu texts which also attack Brāhmaṇical pretensions. Lastly, these texts illustrate the style in which polemics flourished on a level which did not require of their audience an expertise in *nyāya-śāstra.*

With the literature ascribed to Aśvaghoṣa and other early Buddhist writers, the same sort of difficulties with regard to authorship and date which were experienced with the earlier literature persist nearly to an equal degree. Aśvaghoṣa's case exemplifies these problems well. Today, most authorities agree that Aśvaghoṣa could well have been a contemporary of Kaṇiṣka (*c.* A.D. 78-101). Yet, this opinion has been called into doubt upon study of the *Sūtrālaṅkāra.* There Aśvaghoṣa tells two stories which deal with Kaṇiṣka's reign as though it were in the past.[22] Yet this fact does not rule out the possibility that Aśvaghoṣa flourished in Kaṇiṣka's era, for he could well have outlived this king. Moreover, the correctness of ascribing the *Sūtrālaṅkāra* to Aśvaghoṣa has been the subject of considerable controversy.[23]

Assuming then that Aśvaghoṣa flourished during the later part of the first century A.D., the extraordinary thing about his writings is that a pair of them reveal a fully-developed *kāvya* style, albeit one free from the ornate complexities which mark later works in the genre. Aśvaghoṣa apparently felt that it might be viewed as a curious phenomenon that he as a Buddhist monk should have recourse to the seductive charms of the *mahākāvya* in order to preach his religion. Yet he apparently felt that mankind was for the most part too obsessed with the pursuit of mundane pleasures to heed straightaway the Buddhist call to a life of renunciation. Therefore, at the very end of his *Saundarananda*, an entertaining tale of a reluctant conversion to the monastic life, Aśvaghoṣa reveals that his true purpose has been to bring men to the peace of liberation (*mokṣa*), rather than merely to provide them entertainment. Without the delights of *kāvya*, he asks, how else might he ensnare the minds of his distracted audience? Thus, his bitter advice has been sweetened so that it might be palatable and able, therefore, to benefit mankind, as a bitter medicine mixed with honey.[24]

Brāhmaṇical Ethics

Before taking up the matter of the *Vajrasūcī* and Aśvaghoṣa's disputed authorship of it, it seems appropriate to provide some background to the anti-Brāhmaṇism which marks this and a fair number of other Buddhist and Jaina texts.

Much of the heterodox criticism of Brāhmaṇas must be attributed to the Brāhmaṇical ethic as it evolved through the Vedic, Sūtra and Epic eras. The first mention of a division of society into classes known as Brāhmaṇas, Kṣatriyas, Vaiśyas and Śūdras occurs in a late hymn of the *Ṛgveda* known as the 'Puruṣa-Sūkta' (X.90.11-12). That reference, with its association of the various classes with various bodily organs beginning with the mouth and descending through the arms, thighs, and feet, clearly suggests that the same hierarchical order so familiar in later times was a characteristic of Āryan society even then. However, controversy arises over the question of the degree of rigidity possessed by the class structure of that time. Those who argue for a relatively open and flexible class structure in Vedic times draw our attention to the silence of the *Ṛgveda*, despite its great length, in defining the rights, duties, privileges and other matters constituting codes of conduct for each class which so mark the later *Smṛti* literature. They also point to literary evidence within the *Ṛgveda* itself which indicates that the class system was not yet a function of hereditary succession. Thus, various occupations which would suit members of distinct classes in later times are seen in the *Ṛgveda* to be engaged in by members of a single family (IX.92.3). Lastly, it is noted that inter-dining and inter-marriage were a common practice then.[25]

Yet, even if there did exist a relatively open class system in the period of the *Ṛgveda*, the evidence of the *Brāhmaṇas*, then, shows a clear progression towards an iron-clad rigidity. In these texts it would be enjoined that only Brāhmaṇas were entitled to receive a full education; Kṣatriyas and Vaiśyas were entitled to progressively more limited education; a Śūdra was entitled to none. Moreover, women were consigned to an abysmal status.[26] The same period saw the imposition of increasingly elaborate codes of behaviour upon each of the three lower groups from the priests above them. Thus, the social mobility of the three lower groups was diminished along with the regimentation of their behaviour. The priests, for their part, continued to elaborate the complexity of their ritual and its theoretical bases to an almost unbelievable degree. This, no doubt, effected an appreciation of the market value of their rites while making it virtually impossible for an outsider to pretend to the expertise so jealously guarded within their guild. S.C. Crawford describes the resultant ethical milieu as follows:

> Judged in isolation, these rules seemed merely decorative, but their cumulative effect was socially destructive. They helped create a climate in which each caste was reminded in a myriad miniscule manners of the place it occupied in the hierarchical order of society. The rationale for some of these distinctions was purportedly ethical, but its underlying concept of sin had no basis in ethics.[27]

Illustrative of this last point, we might take note of the ritual defilement imposed upon one guilty of spitting upon a Brāhmaṇa: to be lodged, in the after-life 'in the middle of a stream running with blood, devouring hair'.[28] So it happened that the caste system became solidified, and, as Crawford puts it, 'intoxicated the Brahmins with delusions of godliness'.[29] Also, 'If divinity were the norm of impartial justice, the Brahmins may be respected as the embodiments of the moral order; instead, the Brahmins interpreted their divine status to mean that law served them—they did not have to serve the law'.[30] If it be objected that the *Smṛtis* imposed more rigorous punishments upon the Brāhmaṇas than the lower classes for the commission of the same offense, it is nonetheless true that the Brāhmaṇas received preferential treatment in practice. Thus, a Brāhmaṇa violating the wife of a Śūdra would fare better than a Śūdra violating the wife of a Brāhmaṇa.[31] 'The real height of contempt and exorbitant self-importance is reached in the law which ordinarily forbids a Brahmin to give left-over food to non-Brahmins, but this law is waived, provided the Brahmin "shall clean his teeth and give the food after having placed in it the dirt from his teeth".'[32]

In the light of this evidence of the Brāhmaṇas' institutionalized degradation of the inferior classes, we are now in a much improved position to follow Max-Müller's explanation of the Buddha's success: 'it was sufficient that one man should challenge the authority of the Brāhmaṇas. . .and preach among the scorned and degraded creatures of God the simple truth that salvation was possible without the mediation of priests, and without a belief in books to which these very priests had given the title of revelation.'[33] The challenge which Buddhist authors most often presented in their polemics is concerned with the qualifications for Brāhmaṇahood, especially the belief that the matter is determinable by one's birth.

Although any number of verses in Epic and pre-Classical Sanskrit literature glorify Brāhmaṇas and Brāhmaṇahood,[34] the question of what makes a man an authentic Brāhmaṇa, with all the spiritual pre-eminence implied in that term, is nevertheless raised every now and then in Hindu texts of the same period and later. The grammarian Patañjali quotes the following verse:

Tapaḥ śrutaṃ ca yoniś cetyetad brāhmaṇakārakam |
Tapaḥśrutābhyāṃ yo hīno jātibrāhmaṇa eva saḥ ||[35]

'Austerity, learning and birth: these make a Brāhmaṇa; lacking austerity and learning, one is a Brāhmaṇa only by birth.'

The Arguments of the Vajrasūcī

Such thoughts are amplified in the sterner arguments of the

Buddhist *Vajrasūcī*, a work most often attributed to Aśvaghoṣa. The *Vajrasūcī* delivers a sweeping attack on orthodox opinion as to what constitutes Brāhmaṇahood. An interesting aspect of the work is that it borrows extensively from such revered sources of Brāhmaṇical tradition as the Vedas, the *Mahābhārata* and the *Manusmṛti* in support of its unorthodox solutions to the problem of what makes an authentic Brāhmaṇa. If the gnomic verse quoted in Patañjali's *Mahābhāṣya* implies that a Brāhmaṇa by birth who lacks austerity and learning is an inferior Brāhmaṇa, the *Vajrasūcī* would surely imply that such an individual is no Brāhmaṇa at all. It notes that Kapila, Viśvāmitra and others are reputed to have actually become Brāhmaṇas without having been born to Brāhmaṇa mothers. But if it be objected that a Brāhmaṇa father alone suffices to produce a Brāhmaṇa child, then the *Vajrasūcī* finds it inconsistent that the community of the Brāhmaṇas should refuse to accept into their fold the offspring of servant girls made pregnant by their Brāhmaṇa masters. For that matter, the Brāhmaṇical status of each and every Brāhmaṇa may be called into question when it is recalled that from very ancient times the wives of Brāhmaṇas have been observed to form non-sanctioned unions with men of even the lowest castes. Manu's declaration that upon the commission of an act incurring ritual impurity, such as selling milk or meat, a Brāhmaṇa is immediately transformed into a Śūdra itself conflicts with the opinion that birth alone is sufficient to make a Brāhmaṇa. Can all the wickedness of a bad horse change him into a pig? And if it be claimed that something so corporeal as birth to Brāhmaṇa parents insures Brāhmaṇahood, then the very sacred fire, so often personified as a priest itself, then commits the heinous sin of slaying a Brāhmaṇa during the funeral rites. If it be claimed that Brāhmaṇahood is a function of education, then even learned demons like Rāvaṇa must be declared Brāhmaṇas. If the criteria are expertise and the capacity to teach, then, obviously, many Śūdras are under-ranked.

What are the *Vajrasūcī*'s criteria for Brāhmaṇahood? They are truth, austerity, self-control and compassion for all sentient creatures.[36]

The Authorship of the Vajrasūcī

It might well be asked if the aims of the *Vajrasūcī* are indeed as gentle as declared in this last statement: namely, the appeal to truthfulness and so forth. After all, it could not be published in the last century without the appended 'refutation' of the *paṇḍita* who cooperated in editing the text;[37] it seems that the text is still capable of piquing Brāhmaṇas. The text is clearly designed to challenge Brāhmaṇical pretensions to inherited spiritual nobility. This fact alone has caused some question to arise concerning the traditional ascription of the *Vajrasūcī* to Aśvaghoṣa, whom some historians consider to be of Brāhmaṇical parentage. Winternitz flatly states that 'It may be taken as certain that he [Aśvaghoṣa] was of Brāhmaṇa family, and had enjoyed a thorough Brāhmaṇical education before he went over to Buddhism.'[38] Winternitz finds confirmation of this tradition in the 'abundant allusions to Brāhmaṇical legends and epic narratives' in Aśvaghoṣa's *Buddhacarita* and *Saundarananda*.[39] In the introduction to the second part of his translation of the *Buddhacarita*, E.H. Johnston also stresses Aśvaghoṣa's intimate familiarity with Brāhmaṇical mythology, especially as found in the *Rāmāyaṇa*. Johnston also notes that Aśvaghoṣa twice stresses the descent of the Śākya clan of the Buddha from the Ikṣvāku dynasty and further notes that Aśvaghoṣa displays expertise in a wide range of Brāhmaṇical lore, including the Vedas and other ritual texts.[40] The problem, then, confronting the historians of Sanskrit literature, is whether or not the anti-Brāhmaṇism of the *Vajrasūcī* can be reconciled with Aśvaghoṣa's supposed Brāhmaṇical education. Indeed, even beyond the Brāhmaṇical erudition to be found in Aśvaghoṣa's accepted works, S.K. De finds that in them 'everywhere great respect is shown to Brāhmaṇical ideas and institutions' and doubts Aśvaghoṣa's alleged authorship of the *Vajrasūcī*, declaring that, 'it shows little of Aśvaghoṣa's style or mentality'.[41]

Now it seems to me that Brāhmaṇical erudition and a critical view of the frailty of the Brāhmaṇas' caste-pretensions are not irreconcilable. We have already seen how the author of the *Vajrasūcī* also utilizes a thorough familiarity with Brāhmaṇical texts, but for his own purposes. As an early translator describes the text: 'what adds to its pungency is that throughout the truth of the Brāhmaṇical writings is assumed, and that the author's proofs of the erroneousness of the doctrine of caste are all drawn from those writings. He possesses himself of the enemy's battery, and turns their own guns against them.'[42] Winternitz adds the following: 'For the sake of the quotations from Brāhmaṇical texts, if on no other grounds, this work would be of great importance in the history of literature. . . .'[43] So it would appear that the Brāhmaṇical erudition which the *Buddhacarita*, the *Saundarananda* and the *Vajrasūcī* have in common would support the claim that Aśvaghoṣa composed all three. If the style of the *Vajrasūcī* strikes S.K. De as dissimilar from that of Aśvaghoṣa's acknowledged works, I think it relevant to point out that the other works are *mahākāvyas* after all, and who would expect the elegant niceties of a *mahākāvya* to find their way into a ten-page broadside? De also accuses the *Vajrasūcī* of showing little of Aśvaghoṣa's 'mentality'. To this charge, I think it might be replied that it is a fairly simple matter to admire the high points of Brāhmaṇical culture without sharing Brāhmaṇical social prejudices; moreover, it seems improbable to me that this simple distinction could not be drawn by a Buddhist—*especially* by a Buddhist who left the ranks of the Brāhmaṇas to join the *Saṅgha*.

Among the historians, only S.K. De seems to think that the *Vajrasūcī*'s criticism of Brāhmaṇas argues against Aśvaghoṣa's authorship of the same text. Winternitz, however, does admit 'some serious objections to ascribing the authorship to Aśvaghoṣa': "The *Vajrasūcī* is not enumerated either by I-tsing or in the Tibetan Tanjur among the works of Aśvaghoṣa; and in the catalogues of the Chinese Tripiṭaka a Vajrasūcī, which is said to contain 'a refutation of the four Vedas', and which was translated into Chinese between A.D., 973 and 981 is ascribed to a man named Dharmakīrti."[44] But in his recent study of both the Sanskrit text and the Chinese version, Sujitkumar Mukhopadhyaya finds that sufficient evidence does exist to ascribe the work to Aśvaghoṣa. Of the several arguments which Mukhopadhyaya presents, the most relevant to Winternitz's objections is one which notes that the Chinese translation is quite obscure and corrupt. He concludes that that version is, in all likelihood, an *adaptation* of the original text by Dharmakīrti—a suggestion first made by Sylvain Lévi in the *Journal Asiatique* in 1908.[45] As for the argument that the work is not cited by either I-tsing or the Tibetan Tanjur as being among the works of Aśvaghoṣa, Mukhopadhyaya notes that neither the *Saundarananda* nor the

Śāriputra-prakaraṇa—both widely accepted as works of Aśvaghoṣa—are mentioned in either of these Chinese or Tibetan sources.[46]

The Sūtrālaṅkāra

The controversy surrounding the fragmentary *Sūtrālaṅkāra* and its ascription to Aśvaghoṣa has been alluded to above.[47] Although the work may have been composed, or at least refashioned, by another Buddhist author, it shares with the *Vajrasūcī* an erudite knowledge of Brāhmaṇical texts and a critical view of Brāhmaṇical social thought. The text mentions the *Rāmāyaṇa*, the *Mahābhārata*, the Sāṅkhya and Vaiśeṣika systems, Jaina doctrines and the *Manusmṛti*; in the same way that the *Vajrasūcī* used such texts to criticize Brāhmaṇical elitism, so does the *Sūtrālaṅkāra*, but in the context of moral tales similar to those of the *Jātaka* and *Avadāna* collections and told in an ornate *kāvya* style.

Reflections in the Pali Literature

Now that we have considered a Buddhist attack upon Brāhmaṇical social thought as represented by the Sanskrit *Vajrasūcī*, it might be useful to take note of two of several parallels which occur in the Pali literature. The two Pali texts to be examined in this connection are the *Soṇadaṇḍa-sutta* and the *Dhammapada*. Like the *Vajrasūcī*, both texts address themselves to the definition of characteristics of the true Brāhmaṇa.

In the *sutta* which bears his name, Soṇadaṇḍa is portrayed as a learned Brāhmaṇa who comes to an interview with the Buddha, though somewhat apprehensive that he might appear a fool if unable to skilfully exchange questions and answers with the Enlightened One. As it happens, Soṇadaṇḍa is much relieved when asked a question the answer of which he feels he knows with certainty: a question requiring him to define those characteristics by which one may accurately claim to be a Brāhmaṇa. Soṇadaṇḍa replies that there are five such characteristics: pure descent through seven generations; mastery of the three Vedas and their ancillary literature; endowment with certain physical characteristics [which proclaim his race]; virtuousness; and, wisdom.

When asked by the Buddha if all five of these characteristics are absolutely necessary for a man to possess in order to say accurately that he is a Brāhmaṇa, Soṇadaṇḍa admits that physical characteristics (literally, colour) are not essential to make a true Brāhmaṇa. When pressed further, Soṇadaṇḍa admits that mastery of the Vedas is not essential to Brāhmaṇa-hood. Pressed further still, Soṇadaṇḍa admits that even pure lineage is not essential. At this point, Soṇadaṇḍa's Brāhmaṇa colleagues object that he has undervalued their colour, Vedic learning and birth. Soṇadaṇḍa replies that colour, Vedic verses and birth do little to avail one who kills, steals, tells lies, commits adultery and so forth. Therefore, he concludes as before that virtue and wisdom alone make a Brāhmaṇa. As a test, the Buddha asks Soṇadaṇḍa if he is prepared to concede that either virtue or wisdom is non-essential to make a true Brāhmaṇa. This time Soṇadaṇḍa replies in the negative, declaring that virtue and wisdom are co-extensive and that each purifies the other.

Soṇadaṇḍa has answered all the Buddha's questions admirably. He has, moreover, through the Buddha's gentle probing, stripped away the elitist superficialities and arrived at a clear view of which characteristics are essential to a true Brāhmaṇa. In what the Buddhist author of this *sutta* must have seen as a reasonable consequence to Soṇadaṇḍa's discovery, the latter is depicted in the final scene of the text as taking refuge in the Buddha, the *Dharma* and the *Saṅgha*. Finally, in a remarkable anti-climax, Soṇadaṇḍa, apparently still anxious to maintain his status in the Brāhmaṇical community, explains in some detail to the Buddha his intention not to pay him the public veneration due to him.[48]

The final chapter of the *Dhammapada* is devoted solely to the definition of the characteristics of a true Brāhmaṇa. Its forty-one verses are of the gnomic variety, thus bringing it closer to the *Vajrasūcī* in style; but it remains closer to the *Soṇadaṇḍa-sutta* in tone: remonstrating with the Brāhmaṇas rather than baiting them. But if the chapter lacks the virulence of the *Vajra-sūcī*, still, the following pair of verses judges with some severity the hypocrisy of the Brāhmaṇas' concern to wear an assumed holiness designed to mask inner corruption:

A man does not become a Brāhmaṇa by matted hair, or

> gotra or birth. One in whom there is truth, dharma and purity is indeed a Brāhmaṇa.
>
> O Fool, what is the use of your matted locks? What good is your black-antelope skin? There is a morass within you, [yet,] it is the outside which you punctiliously preen![49]

A real Brāhmaṇa should be absolutely independent, even from the (Brāhmaṇical) gods:

> I term him a Brāhmaṇa who, after casting off his ties to men, has left behind his ties to heaven and is free from all ties.[50]

Neither birth nor privilege, but ethics make a true Brāhmaṇa:

> I do not term him a Brāhmaṇa by birth or mother, who speaks condescendingly and is wealthy. I call a Brāhmaṇa one who has nothing and takes nothing from others.[51]

One of the characteristics of such gnomic verses as the above is that they are apt to be requoted often in later literature; moreover, one is never altogether certain that the verse before one's eyes is not itself borrowed from some earlier source. Winternitz noted that more than half of the total verses of the *Dhammapada* had been traced to other texts in the Pali canon.[52] Since the work belongs to the fifth and latest *nikāya* of the *Sutta-piṭaka*, it would seem quite possible that such verses antedate their inclusion in the *Dhammapada*. Even more interesting with regard to tracing the original literary sources of these criticisms is Winternitz's statement that 'the collection [of sayings in the *Dhammapada*] has come to include some sayings which were *originally not Buddhist at all*, but were drawn from that inexhaustible source of Indian gnomic wisdom, from which they also found their way into Manu's law-book, into the *Mahābhārata*, the texts of the Jains, and into narrative works such as the *Pañcatantra*, etc.'[53] And, in noting the difficulty of determining where such sayings first appeared, Winternitz adds that 'Brahmanical sources may occasionally be assumed.'[54]

The Cittaviśuddhiprakaraṇam

The Brāhmaṇical notion of the removal of sin through the practice of ritual bathing in the river Gaṅgā (Ganges) is ridiculed in a short Buddhist work called the *Cittaviśuddhiprakaraṇam*,

'(On) the Subject of the Purification of the Mind', at first attributed to the well-known philosopher of the third century A.D., Āryadeva.[55] In it, the author notes that even though an impure clay vessel be washed repeatedly with water, still it remains tainted, implying that a wicked man's repeated ritual ablutions will avail him no more. He adds that a dog will not gain purity in the waters of the Gaṅgā, and declares sarcastically that the sacred bathing of 'religiously-minded' men must therefore be fruitless. And if *dharma* is determined by bathing, then (lowly) fishermen must have gained perfection, not to mention the fish and the other water-creatures which are immersed in water day and night! Observing that attachment and so forth continue to plague the minds of those who worship at sacred bathing spots, the author concludes that the expiation of sins is impossible through ritual bathing.[56]

References

1. Cited by S.N. Dasgupta, *HSLCP*, p. xiv.
2. Ibid., pp. xiii-xiv.
3. Ibid., p. xvii.
4. Loc. cit.
5. Loc. cit.
6. Ibid., p. xvi.
7. *MB*, 1697, commenting on Pāṇini's *taddhita sūtra 'tena proktam'*, 4.3.101; vol. II of the Delhi (1967) edition. The exact citation is on p. 461.
8. *MB*, 243, commenting on Pāṇini's '*Yū stryākhyau nadī*', 1.4.3; vol. I, pp. 217ff. of the Delhi (1967) edition. The quote is on p. 219.
9. Keith, *HSL*, pp. 45-47.
10. Staal, *RSG*, p. 78, referring to Erich Frauwallner, 'Sprachtheorie und Philosophie im Mahābhāṣyam des Patañjali', *WZKSOA*, 3, pp. 92–118.
11. J.W. de Jong, *IIJ*, vol. XVI, no. 3 (1975), p. 229, citing Poussin, *L'Inde aux temps des Mauryas*, Paris, 1930, pp. 199-202.
12. *IHQ*, vol. VII, 1931, pp. 724ff.
13. *Indian Culture*, vol. VI, pp. 110ff.
14. Müller, *HASL*, p. 452.
15. Ibid., pp. 453-54.
16. Gonda in *Orientalia Neederlandica*, Leiden, 1948, p. 314: citing Haug, Brahma und die Brahmanen, Munchen 1871, p. 12.
17. Ibid., p. 315. For concurring opinions, Gonda refers his readers to the following sources: M. Bloomfield, *JAOS*, 17 (1896), pp. 173ff.; H.H. Bender, *JAOS*, 37, pp. 186ff.; W. Norman Brown, *NIA*, 2, pp. 115ff; Bächtold-Stäubli, in *Hand-wörterbuch des deutschen Aberglaubens*, 3, p. 125, 129; H. Oldenberg, *Die Religion des Veda*, p. 68.

18. S.K. De, *WHS*, p. 158, citing *SB*, 14.1.1.32 and *MS*, 10.27.12.
19. Trans. A.B. Keith, *The Ṛig-Veda Brāhmaṇas, HOS*, 25, p. 300.
20. De, loc. cit.
21. Gonda, op. cit., p. 348.
22. Keith, *HSL*, p. 55.
23. De, *HSLCP*, p. 72, notes this controversy and refers readers to Tomomatsu in *JA*, 1931, II, p. 135ff., also L. de la Valee Poussin, *Vijñaptimātra*[*tā*]-*siddhi*, pp. 221-24.
24. Cf. the two final verses of the *Saundarananda*, edited by Haraprasād Śāstrī: *Ityeṣā vyupaśāntaye na rataye Mokṣārtha-garbhākṛtiḥ, Śrotṛṇāṃ grahaṇārthamanyamanasāṃ kāvyopacārātkṛtā/ Yanmokṣātkṛtamanyadatra hi mayā tatkāvyadharmmātkṛtam, Pātum tiktamivauṣadhaṃ madhuyutaṃ hṛdyaṃ kathaṃ syāditi//* (63) *Prāyeṇālokya lokaṃ viṣayaratiparaṃ mokṣāt pratihataṃ, Kāvyavyājena tattvaṃ kathitamiha mayā mokṣaparamiti/..//* (64). Calcutta, *Bibliotheca Indica*, 1939, p. 126.
25. S. Cromwell Crawford, *The Evolution of Hindu Ethical Ideas*, Calcutta, 1974, pp. 21-24.
26. Cf. A.B. Keith, *Religion and Philosophy of the Veda, HOS*, vol. 32 (1925), p. 475:

> A final proof of the brutal morality of the priest can be adduced in the position assigned to women: woman in India has always suffered much from all religions, but by none has she been so thoroughly despised as by the Brahmans of the period of the Brahmanas.

Quoted, Crawford, ibid., p. 43.

27. Crawford, op. cit., p. 49.
28. Ibid., p. 50.
29. Loc. cit.
30. Loc. cit.
31. Ibid., p. 83.
32. Ibid., pp. 83-84.
33. Müller, op. cit., quoted on p. 3 of the Introduction above.
34. Cf. the *Anugītā* section of the *Mahābhārata*. D.D. Kosambi considers the former to be a later interpolation, Cf. his *Myth and Reality*, p. 18.
35. Quoted in Keith, *HSL*, p. 46.
36. Sujitkumar Mukhopadhyaya, *The Vajrasūcī of Aśvaghoṣa* (Revised Second Edition), Śāntiniketan, 1960, pp. vi-x and 1-11.
37. Ibid., p. xvi, n. 2.
38. *HIL*, vol. II, p. 257.
39. Ibid., p. 265.
40. E.H. Johnston, *The Buddhacarita: or, Acts of the Buddha*, reprinted, Delhi: 1972, Introduction to Part II, pp. xv-xviii.
41. *HSLCP*, pp. 70-71.
42. B.H. Hodgson, *Wujra Soochi or Refutation of the Arguments upon which the Brahmanical Institution of Caste is Founded*, Calcutta, 1839; this same quote can be found in the *Transactions of the the Royal Asiatic Society of Great Britain and Ireland*, vol. III, London, 1839; cited in Mukhopadhyaya, op. cit., pp. xiv, 25.

43. Winternitz, op. cit., p. 266.
44. Winternitz, loc. cit.,
45. *JA*, 1908: *S*. 10, T. XII, p. 71.
46. Mukhopadhyaya, op. cit., pp. xi-xv.
47. Vide above, n. 23. Cf. also H. Lüders, *Bruchstücke der Kalpanāmaṇḍitikā des Kumāralāta* in Kongel Preuss Turfan-Expeditionen, Kleinere Sanskrit-Texte II, Leipzig, 1926.
48. Cf. *Dialogues of the Buddha*, translated from the Pali by T.W. Rhys Davids, in *Sacred Books of the Buddhists*, edited by F. Max-Müller, vol. II, pp. 137–59.
49. *The Dhammapada*, 26.11-12 (393-94).
50. Ibid., 26.35 (417).
51. Ibid., 26.14 (396).
52. *HIL*, vol. II, p. 83.
53. *HIL*, vol. II, p. 84 (underscoring added).
54. Ibid., fn. 2.
55. That the work belonged to the famous Āryadeva was first declared by Haraprasād Sāstrī (*cf.* 'The Discovery of a Work by Āryadeva in Sanskrit', *Journal of the Asiatic Society of Bengal*, LXVII [1898], pp. 175–84), an opinion shared by H. Jacobi, (*JAOS*, 31, 1910, p. 2), and by A.B. Keith (*HSL*, p. 71) who confuses it with the *Catuḥśataka;* a confusion continued in S.C. Banerji's *A Companion to Sanskrit Literature*, p. 175. Later Sāstrī noted that the close of the piece contained ideas and expressions anachronistic to the great Āryadeva's time and was led to conclude that 'The book has been revised by another Āryadeva in later times. . .' (*Indian Historical Quarterly*, vol. I, [1925], p. 464).
56. The *Cittaviśuddhiprakaraṇam*, vv. 60-64, printed in H. P. Śāstrī, 'Discovery of a Work by Āryadeva', *JBRAS*, LXVII, 1898, p. 180.

Chapter 2

THE IDEALIZATION OF LIFE AND SOCIAL CRITICISM IN THE CLASSICS

The idealization of life which marks the compositions of Kālidāsa and his fellow *mahākavis* is doubtless one of the principal reasons why social criticism is so seldom associated with Sanskrit literature. Yet, I hope to show that a significant strain of social criticism runs through some of the best known and most often read Sanskrit classics.

Kālidāsa's World

In the case of even the most celebrated of Sanskrit poets, Kālidāsa, the now-familiar difficulties of assigning even an approximate date and place again confront historians of Sanskrit literature. Over the years, remarkably disparate estimates of Kālidāsa's date have been put forward. Writing in 1897, Gopal Raghunath Nandargikar brings no less than 165 pages of argumentation to a close with the statement that 'from these proofs we have no hesitation to place Kālidāsa somewhere between 300 B.C. and 100 B.C.'[1] But, writing some 31 years later, A.B. Keith concludes that 'Kālidāsa then lived before A.D. 472, and probably at a considerable distance, so that to place him about A.D. 400 seems completely justified.'[2]

Kālidāsa's writings reveal a marked contrast to the anti-Brāhmaṇical sentiment found in the Buddhist works considered at the close of the last chapter. Far from criticizing Brāhmaṇical social thought, Kālidāsa creates a poetic milieu in which the Brāhmaṇical world view forms the basis of an idealized life. *Āśramas* and villages where the air is pungent with smoke issuing from sacrificial fires into which Brāhmaṇas constantly offer oblations are found in the *Raghuvaṃśa* and the *Abhijñānaśākuntalam*. In two places in the *Raghuvaṃśa* a Brāhmaṇa's blessing is instrumental to a king's obtaining a son and heir. A king milks the earth to obtain materials to offer the gods through the medium of the Brāhmaṇa's sacrificial fires; and Indra, thus propitiated, milks the storm clouds to provide the rains necessary to the agricultural economy. The idealized societies under the Raghu monarchs swerve not from the noble rut established by Manu. Citizens and kings pursue the legitimate aims of religion, wealth, pleasure and ultimate liberation (the *caturvarga*). All are mindful of the duties arising from their caste and stage of life (their *varṇāśramadharma*).[3] In the person of Rāmacandra, Viṣṇu himself finds embodiment. The divine union of Śiva and Pārvatī is celebrated in the *Kumārasaṃbhava*, and prayers are addressed to Viṣṇu and Brahmā in the same poem. The Kaṇva and Vaśiṣṭha *ṛṣis* are portrayed with deference and awe. The model wives, Sītā and Pārvatī, have recourse to asceticism (*tapasyā*) in order to win union with their beloveds in this or the next life. That Kālidāsa's works are steeped in Brāhmaṇical lore is proved by references in the poems to principles of the Sāṅkhya, Yoga, Mīmāṃsā and Vedānta systems, together with further references to *śāstras* expounding astrology (*jyotiṣa*), polity (*nīti*), medicine (*āyurveda*), grammar (*vyākaraṇa*) and sexual science (*kāmaśāstra*). Kālidāsa's Hindu kings are for the most part paradigms of regal rectitude, forebearance and bravery. Although a modern Western reader may find Kālidāsa's portrayal of King Agnimitra as an aged swain scurrying about oblivious to affairs of state with the twofold aim of winning the youthful Mālavikā and avoiding detection by his queen as absurdly farcical, it should be remembered that Kālidāsa's Indian admirers have never found it so. In the *Mālavikāgnimitram*, as S. K. De puts it, 'we have polite banter, witty compliments and frivolous philandering, but no satire or caricature appears to have been meant.'[4] So much does Kālidāsa legitimize the manifold amorous proclivities of his Raghu kings that we cannot be entirely certain of satirical intent even in his portrayal of King Agnivarṇa, who is so devoted to his harem that he finds himself too preoccupied to grant his subjects interviews, and, instead, hangs his lotus foot out of a window to receive their kisses![5]

As Kālidāsa is mentioned in an inscription at Aihole dated to A.D. 634, we can feel certain that he lived no later than the seventh century. In the same inscription is mentioned another celebrated Sanskrit poet named Bhāravi. Like Kālidāsa, Bhāravi chose an incident from one of the great epics to depict in a *Mahākāvya*, the *Kirātārjunīyam*. Again like Kālidāsa, Bhāravi depicts a milieu in which Brāhmaṇical ideals and the acceptance of Brāhmaṇical theology goes unquestioned. In fact, in the sixth and seventh centuries, three other eminent Sanskrit poets followed the lead of Kālidāsa and Bhāravi in selecting tales from the *Rāmāyaṇa* and the *Mahābhārata* to celebrate in their *mahākāvyas*. While Bhāravi introduced the new element of grammatical *tours de force* in his *Kirātārjunīyam*, Māgha attempted to overshadow his predecessor in this manneristic predilection in his *Śiśupālavadham*. The story of the *Rāmāyaṇa* was retold twice more in Kumāradāsa's *Jānakīharaṇam*, a work sometimes said to rival Kālidāsa's poetry, and in a work by the poet Bhaṭṭi titled the *Rāvaṇavadham* but popularly known as the *Bhaṭṭikāvyam*. Ostensibly written for the purpose of illustrating the principles of Sanskrit grammar, the *Bhaṭṭikāvyam* so develops the trend to displays of recondite facets of grammar that its author boasts that his poem is only *vyākhyā-gamyam*, that is, understandable solely with the aid of a commentary. That each of these poets should have chosen to retell the worn and rather trite stories of the epics is understandable when one considers that the authors were in all likelihood inspired by the wish to pay homage to the Hindu gods whose adventures are depicted in the poems, rather than by the desire to capture the interest of their audience with novel stories. This devotional factor in the composition of Sanskrit *kāvyas* is observable throughout all subsequent eras of Sanskrit poetry even to the present time when *mahākāvyas* retelling the story of Rāma and Sītā and the stories of Kṛṣṇa and the *gopīs* are still being written and published.

Society in the Mṛcchakaṭika

Turning to one noteworthy example of the early Sanskrit drama, we find a good deal more social realism and even elements of social criticism in the *Mṛcchakaṭika* of Śūdraka. Here, much more than in later Sanskrit dramas, we find both plot and characters drawn from real life. In a word, the play is *laukika*. Although sufficient respect is shown to Brāhmaṇas, Śūdraka did not conform to the trend whichever presented them as paradigms of *dhārmic* rectitude rarely seen away from their sacred fires. His hero, Cārudatta, is a married Brāhmaṇa whose falling in love with a courtesan forms the focal point of the play. In spite of this, and in spite of the fact that we learn that Cārudatta's forefathers accumulated a considerable fortune by stooping to engage in commerce (as *sārthavāhas*),[6] Cārudatta is portrayed sympathetically as so generous that he has been rendered penniless by his many charities. Another poor Brāhmaṇa, Śarvilaka, is shown delighting in his skill as a thief, an occupation he has adopted in order to buy the freedom of his enslaved beloved. The third impoverished Brāhmaṇa is a *vidūṣaka*, Maitreya, who is a refreshing contrast to the mindless glutton we usually find in this stock role. As his name implies, Maitreya is an honest and sincere friend to Cārudatta.

And if there is realism in the depiction of the play's Brāhmaṇas, there is a real element of social criticism in the view we get of the king and his villainous brother-in-law, Saṃsthānaka (Śakāra). Although King Pālaka never appears on the stage, the playwright leaves no doubt that he is a merciless tyrant. The play's happy resolution involves a successful revolution in which the king is overthrown by the noble Āryaka. Before this event, we learn such interesting facts about the condition of society under the evil rule as, for example, that of the doubtfulness of a fair trial for a man too poor to buy his innocence (this doubt is given as one of the reasons for the falsely accused Cārudatta's failure to defend himself adequately at his trial). We also learn that a prisoner convicted of no less than a capital offense had the option of ransoming his freedom if he could raise enough money. We also learn that a creditor was entitled to inflict corporal punishment upon his debtors or to sell them into slavery. And, if there was a doubt concerning the guilt or innocence of a man placed on trial, he could be compelled to 'prove' his innocence by withstanding the following ordeals: (1) poison; (2) being held under water while a runner pursued and retrieved an arrow shot from a bow; (3) remaining unhurt in the midst of a fire kindled after the performance of some rituals.[7] The royal court is compared, in an extended analogy, to a sea infested with sharks and crocodiles in the form of spies, and with snakes in the form of bureaucrats (Kāyasthas). The sight of Buddhist monks is deemed inauspicious by proper Hindus, and inter-caste enmity surfaces in the form of insults. Drinking, gambling, prostitution and slavery were widespread. Yet, Śūdraka's foremost indictment of the corrupt ruling family is to be found in his characterization of Saṃsthānaka (Śakāra). An out and out villain who trades upon his close connection with the king, Śakāra is portrayed as a conniving coward, lecher and fool. He is a lisping braggart smitten with fanciful notions of his own importance; a bully who attempts murder and succeeds in manipulating the conviction of an innocent man.

Superstition, Hypocrisy and Corruption as Depicted in the Daśakumāracarita

The resemblance in terms of milieu and tone of social criticism in Daṇḍin's *Daśakumāracarita* is so close to the same qualities of the *Mṛcchakaṭika* that one scholar was tempted to assign the authorship of the *Mṛcchakaṭika* to Daṇḍin.[8] Daṇḍin's milieu aptly meets the definition of a picturesque romance: the stories detailing the escapades of merry rascals who live by their wits; the stories are episodic in structure, are realistic in manner, and often satiric in intent.[9] Daṇḍin's realism and satiric intent are, as we shall see in some detail in succeeding paragraphs, often deployed in the depiction of superstitions, the hypocrisy of the religious, and the corruption of state administration.

The society Daṇḍin depicts is within the powerful grasp of polymorphous superstition—a fact not unappreciated by the cunning who are ever willing to exploit the gullible. By the time Daṇḍin wrote in the seventh century, Paurāṇic Hinduism formed the basis of the general religious outlook, and the trinity of Brahmā, Viṣṇu, and Śiva was ascendent. Moreover, a whole range of minor deities and odd semi-divinities exerted a powerful influence on the popular mind. Heavenly musicians (*gandharvas*) and nymphs (*apsarās*) were invoked in a number of pacificatory rites mainly for the purposes of blessing the conception and birth of children, situations over which they were thought to preside. Strange creatures called *kinnaras*, endowed with horses' heads and human bodies, and *kimpuruṣas*, with human heads on horses' bodies, were treated as realities. Another group, the *vidyādharas*, were regarded as capable of flight and of changing their form at will. Moreover, Daṇḍin's society was haunted by fears of malignant spirits known as *piśācas*, *rākṣasas*, *brahmarākṣasas*, *yakṣas* and *grahas*. The *piśācas* were the ghosts of departed humans who revenged themselves on the living by haunting the enemies of their previous lives. The *rākṣasas* were demons endowed with the capability of changing form at will. They sometimes took possession of men's bodies, kidnapped women, or spitefully polluted religious rites. Reference is also made in the *Daśakumāracarita* to a particular class of *rākṣasas* conceived to be the departed spirits of sinful Brāhmaṇas, and who were therefore known as *brahmarākṣasas*. The *brahmarākṣasas* are represented as haunting remote places like isolated islands and places deep in the forest. That Indian society took the danger of *brahmarākṣasas* as a reality is proven by a ninth century inscription at the Kāmākṣī temple which tells of the evil possession of a queen by a *brahmarākṣasa*.[10] There were also *vetālas*, who were vampire-like creatures who took possession of corpses and animated them to perform wicked deeds. Attendants of Kubera, the god of wealth, called *yakṣas* were also represented as taking over the bodies of women and harassing or killing their lovers. The *yakṣas* were not universally represented as malignant, however. Daṇḍin tells of a benevolent female *yakṣa* or *yakṣiṇī* named Tārāvalī.[11] Planetary spirits known as *grahas* exercised a malefic influence over men weakened them. The widespread belief in possession by evil spirits brought about a correspondingly widespread reliance on exorcism.[12]

Daṇḍin tells the tale of a charlatan named Kalahakaṇṭaka, who seduces the woman with whom he has fallen in love by convincing her that her husband has fallen under the undermining influence of a *graha*, and is therefore weakened by jaundice to the degree that he will be unable to father a child. Kalahakaṇṭaka convinces her that the only way to dispel the evil influence of the *graha* upon her husband is to enter an empty grove and place her foot in the hand of a magician residing there. She was then to return to her husband and kick him with her charmed foot. This action would supposedly rid her husband of his disease and render him potent to father a son. Needless to say, the superstitious woman is taken in by the ruse. It is worth mentioning here that she had up to this point never laid eyes on the cunning Kalahakaṇṭaka; all previous communications having been carried on through the medium of a Jaina nun or *śramaṇikā*. Daṇḍin here follows a convention we will see much of in following pages: namely, that Jaina and Buddhist 'nuns' are universally pictured as exploiting their supposed status as religious renunciates to gain access to the homes of married women and to act as go-betweens (or *dūtis*) in delivering messages from would-be or actual paramours, or even, in some cases, employed as procuresses (or *kuṭṭinīs*), managing the affairs of one or more prostitutes. Returning to the tale of Kalahakaṇṭaka and his beloved (Nitambavatī), we find Nitambavatī entering the deserted grove by night. The magician she encounters there is, of course, none other than Kalahakaṇṭaka, who seizes a golden ankle bracelet from her proffered foot and slashes her thigh with his knife and flees. A few days later, the cunning Kalahakaṇṭaka displays the stolen ankle bracelet before Nitambavatī's merchant husband who recognizes it and questions Kalahakaṇṭaka about how it happened to come into his possession. The cunning Kalahakaṇṭaka informs the merchant before an assembly of his fellow merchants that he is employed as a guard at the burning ground and happened one night to observe Nitambavatī snatching a half-burnt corpse from the funeral pyre with the intention of desecrating the corpse with witches' rites. He further relates that he tried to prevent the abominable deed by accosting the witch and manages to scratch her thigh with his knife in the struggle. The city elders then declare Nitambavatī to be a *śākinī* and her hapless husband expels her from his house. It is then a simple matter for the hypocrite Kalahakaṇṭaka to win over the homeless Nitambavatī who has been reduced to wandering, distraught and suicidal.[13]

Another proof of the powerful influence of magical or *tāntrika* influences on the people of Daṇḍin's time is the great efficacy ascribed to magical diagrams (*yantras*) and incantations (*mantras*) by characters in the *Daśakumāracarita*. These elements enter into the story of another hypocritical adventurer who exploits popular superstitions in order to win a kingdom and the hand of his beloved. The adventurer is Mantragupta, and he first catches sight of his beloved Kanakalekhā after she has been abducted from her father's palace by a *rākṣasa* and is destined to be sacrificed by an evil *tāntrika* who has reduced that *rākṣasa* to servility by his use of *mantras*.[14] Mantragupta slays the sorcerer and follows his new love back to the capital, only to lose her again when she and her father are captured by the rival Āndhra king. Finding herself the object of the Āndhra king's unwanted amorous attentions, Kanakalekhā cleverly circulates a concocted report that she has fallen under the power of a jealous *yakṣa* who will not permit her to set eyes on another man. Noting the success of Kanakalekhā's ruse—the report reaches Mantragupta's ears that the anxious king has had no luck in dispelling the (non-existent) *yakṣa* even with the combined efforts of thousands of magicians[15]—Mantragupta, not to be outdone by his beloved in preying upon the credulity of the superstitious Āndhra king and his subjects, relates an interesting tale of his own posing as a great ascetic. He tells that he enters Āndhra country and goes into a cemetery where he shams the matted locks of an ascetic by extracting some similar strands from the cavity of an old Śāla tree and affixing them to the crown of his head. He then covered his body with a collection of rags and patched garments, and soon found himself surrounded with disciples, whose loyalty he secured with a few presents. Then, taking up residence near a lotus-filled lake, he also gathered an enthusiastic following of villagers won over by a few cheap magic tricks. The villagers spread the fame of their new-found saint, declaring him to be expert in the secrets of the Vedas and *vedāṅgas* and a master in expounding other *śāstras*. They declared, moreover, that he never spoke anything that was not true; that a few grains of dust from his feet would suffice to cure the incurably diseased; and, that the malefic influence of the *grahas*, which had withstood the powers of all the magicians drawing mystical diagrams (*yantras*) would be instantaneously washed away when a man's head would be purified by the touch of a few drops of his foot-bath. They felt it impossible to measure the extent of his powers, and declared him to be utterly lacking in vanity. And, with the spread of Mantragupta's fame, it is not long before he is respectfully approached by the Āndhra king, still seeking to deliver Kanakalekhā from her possessive *yakṣa*. Our false ascetic received the king while shamming a meditative trance and producing a well-timed demonstration of his supposed knowledge of occult lore. Mantragupta promises to aid the king after three days, which he spends excavating a hiding place in the waters beside the adjacent bathing place. When the king returns, Mantragupta advises him to perform religious rites and to immerse himself in the waters of the lake after dark. The results of the king's pious deeds will, Mantragupta assures him, transform the king's appearance into one of surpassing youthful beauty which will subsequently intimidate the *yakṣa* and win the heart of Kanakalekhā. As a deft touch, Mantragupta informs the king that he, as a wandering ascetic, has already overstayed his allotted time in one place, and will have departed by morning, secure in the knowledge that his good works among the Āndhras have been crowned by extraordinary service to the king; for indeed, not to have so favoured the king would make him liable to censure by noble men (Āryas). Then, while Mantragupta repairs in secret to his watery hiding place, the king obeys his last instructions to the letter: he takes a ritual bath, dons perfume and a white garland, and propitiates the Brāhmaṇas (who are, in the last words of Mantragupta, 'no less than gods on this earth'). Having completed these preliminaries, the king proceeded to the lakeshore in the company of many attendants bearing torches. After the king has immersed himself in the waters of the lake and swam out to the depth of an elephant's height, he is pulled under the surface by Mantragupta, who had shed his ascetic's disguise and lay in wait in his hidden chamber. After strangling and drowning the king and hiding the corpse in the hidden place, Mantragupta achieves his ultimate ploy: he emerges from the lake declaring that he is the late king transformed into the embodiment of youthful beauty, true to the 'departed' ascetic's predictions—a miracle he offers as the ultimate refutation of disbelieving heretics. The conclusion of this story deals with the predictable freeing of Kanakalekhā and her father, and Mantragupta's marriage to Kanakalekhā and subsequent enjoyment of sovereignty and love both achieved through his clever exploitation of the prevailing superstitions among the Āndhras.

Although we see more of false ascetics in the *Daśakumāracarita*, Daṇḍin presents one of his most penetrating satirical sketches of asceticism in the tale of the genuine, though fallible, ascetic named Marīci. In the second chapter of Daṇḍin's actual work,[16] the great sage Marīci himself relates the story of his encounter with the prostitute Kāmamañjarī. The sage was first introduced to the prostitute when the latter rushed to his feet seeking asylum, declaring that she is not destined for worldly pleasures and now seeks to earn the rewards of a righteous life. The prostitute's mother follows close behind and laments to Marīci that her daughter has neglected her proper profession and wasted her long education in the sixty-four arts. In the course of a long discussion of the mother's role in the making of a successful prostitute, the mother again refers to the efficacy of

Buddhist nuns, this time in the business of circulating reports of the girl's comeliness—and availability—among the townspeople. Kāmamañjarī's mother caps her indictment of her daughter with the revelation that her daughter has strayed so far as to become infatuated with a penniless but attractive Brāhmaṇa youth, while rejecting all wealthy suitors and reducing herself and all her entourage to poverty through her callous neglect of duty.[17] Marīci then addresses himself to persuading Kāmamañjarī to apply herself with earnestness to her duty—prostitution!—for by doing so she may attain the rewards of heaven. When she again pleads with the sage to afford her refuge from the worldly life, Marīci agrees to let her stay for a while in the forest with him, thinking she will tire of the life of austerities and once again yearn to rejoin the world. After her kinsmen agree that this is a suitable suggestion under the circumstances, Kāmamañjarī proceeds to win the heart of the ascetic through her charming performance of her duties at the *āśrama*. She then avails herself of the opportunity to discourse on religious subjects with the sage. In discussing the three aims of model Hindu life, Kāmamañjarī declares duty (*dharma*) to be superior to the other pursuits of pleasure (*kāma*) and wealth (*artha*). Urged to continue, Kāmamañjarī notes that the superiority of *dharma* is proved by the fact that *kāma* and *artha* presuppose *dharma*. Moreover, *dharma* pursued in the absence of the other two is still sufficient to guide one to the supreme end of life. But, *dharma*'s greatest strength is that it is not overthrown by small, almost insignificant, incursions in the realms of wealth and pleasure. Then, in one of the most playfully irreverent passages in Sanskrit literature, Daṇḍin has Kāmamañjarī establish her point with a series of examples dealing with the mythological indiscretions of the Hindu gods and saints: Brahmā's pursuit of Tilottamā;[18] Śiva's corruption of thousands of ascetics' wives;[19] Kṛṣṇa's making love to sixteen thousand cowherds' wives;[20] Brahmā's incestual pursuit of his own daughter;[21] Indra's seduction of the sage Gautama's wife, Ahalyā;[22] the moon-god's heinous sin (*mahāpātaka*) of making love to his *guru* Bṛhaspat's wife;[23] the Sun's bestiality with a mare;[24] Vāyu's passion for a monkey's wife, Añjanā (Hanumān's mother);[25] Bṛhaspati's intercourse with the wife of his elder brother;[26] the sage Parāśara's lust for a fisherman's child;[27] Parāśara's son's connections with his brother's wives;[28] and Atri's union with a doe. Moreover, the gods have been guilty of cheating the demons on numerous occasions. And yet, Kāmamañjarī says, men still revere the gods and *ṛṣis* because they know that a few minor indiscretions will never despoil their virtue—such is the superiority of *dharma*! Kāmamañjarī's arguments having demolished all of Marīci's reservations, he forsakes his vows. She then carts him back into the city where the citizens enjoying a festival all behold Marīci attired in the foppish adornments of a suitor and obviously totally subjected to Kāmamañjarī. There, Kāmamañjarī spurns her new-found lover, explaining that she has won a wager through seducing him.

The story of Upahāravarman contains the now familiar elements of a wicked king and subjects taken in by a skilful opportunist through their superstitious faith in the miracles wrought by *mantras*. What makes the story worth the retelling here is Daṇḍin's obvious approval of the kind of ethical relativism suggested in Kāmamañjarī's discourse with Marīci. There can be no doubt that the *śāstras* of the Brāhmaṇas would condemn Upahāravarman outright: for, as we begin the narration of the portion of his tale relevant to our purposes, he has already inaugurated an illicit relationship with the king's beautiful wife, Puṣkarikā. Acting on Upahāravarman's instructions, Puṣkarikā informs her ugly but libidinous husband that there is a means by which he can assume the handsome form depicted in a painting (actually a portrait of Upahāravarman). She relates that an old, well-travelled *tāpasī*, having taken a motherly concern for the queen, has informed her that there is a *mantra* through which a wife will be able to confer the handsome likeness of the portrait upon her husband—if he agrees to fast upon the night of the full moon; approach a sacred fire in an isolated place; offer into the fire a hundred *samidhs* of sandalwood, a hundred of aloewood, some camphor and many handsome garments; confess all his state secrets upon hearing the sound of a bell; and, embrace his wife with eyes closed. When the king readily assents to attempt the fateful transformation, Queen Puṣkarikā, still following Upahāravarman's instructions, feigns jealousy owing to the king's philandering inclinations, and refuses at first to play her role in the rite. After Puṣkarikā is supposedly relieved by the king's insincere vows of fidelity, the report issues forth that the king will be transformed into a handsome youth through the magic of his beloved queen; a plan approved only after receiving the assent of the king's wise counsellors, 'clever as Bṛhaspati himself'. Moreover, the general opinion was that the effort might well succeed: 'for the power of jewels, *mantras* and potions is immeasurable.' So the king and his queen enter the deserted palace grounds and commence to offer the many required oblations into the sacred fire. Using the thick smoke of the sacrificial fire as a screen, Upahāravarman trades places with the queen. He convinces the foolish king that he is still beholding the transformed countenance of Puṣkarikā by cleverly continuing her previously voiced misgivings concerning the king's faithfulness. Convinced by this stratagem, the king eagerly confesses his state secrets in the hope of hastening his own assumption of the handsome form before him. The conclusion comes when Upahāravarman slays the duped monarch and takes both his queen and throne. At the close of the narration of the tale, we get a most enlightening clue to the moral and ethical priorities of Daṇḍin and, presumably, of Daṇḍin's audience in the seventh century. After hearing this tale of adultery, fraud, sacrilege and regicide, Daṇḍin's hero smiles approvingly, and observes that, notwithstanding the means employed, *kāma*, *artha* and even *dharma* were served well by Upahāravarman![29]

If Daṇḍin took an undeniably realistic view of the faults of kings, it can neither be denied that he had a keen eye in assessing the faults of their Brāhmaṇa counsellors. In Viśruta's tale, we have such a penetrating satirical analysis of subjection of kings by their self-serving Brāhmaṇa advisors that Daṇḍin's description deserves quoting in its entirety. The description comes in the speech of an old rascal named Vihārabhadra, who advises the young king Anantavarmā not to fall into the trap of thinking it his duty to learn polity (*rājanīti*) from his Brāhmaṇa counsellors. Vihārabhadra's warning is as follows:

> Sire, whenever by favour of fortune a person is blessed with prosperity, clever rogues, worrying him with various temptations, accomplish their own designs. Thus some, inspiring hopes in him about the supreme felicity to be enjoyed after death, get his head shaved, gird him with a string of holy grass, clothe him in skins, smear his body with butter,

send him to sleep without his supper,[30] and manage to appropriate all his property; there are (other) heretics, more terrible than these, who persuade him to relinquish children, and even life. If there be a person naturally shrewd enough not to let his property slip out of his hands in exchange for such [a] mirage, then there are others who surround him and say—'We can convert even a single cowrie into a lac of coins, destroy all foes without weapons, or make even a single-bodied mortal an emperor, if only one is ready to follow the path we shall show.' And when he asks them what that path is, they reply—'There are four branches of royal knowledge, *viz.*, the three *Vedas*, the practical arts (such as agriculture, commerce etc.), logic with metaphysics, and the science of government. Of these, the first three are vast and bear fruit slowly: let them alone, therefore. Study only the fourth; it has been recently composed by the learned Viṣṇugupta in six thousand stanzas for the use of the King, (Candragupta) Maurya, [and] which, when well studied and put into practice, yields the desired fruit.' Agreeing to do so, the king reads and hears it, and just grows old while doing so. (For) that *śāstra* is connected with others; unless all are read, nothing is thoroughly known! Let its principles be grasped after a short or long time [i.e. let that go]: when this *śāstra* is learnt, the first lesson taught is [this]—'Do not trust one's wife or child.' Regarding the filling of one's belly, the precept is—'So much rice is needed to make up so much boiled rice, and so much fuel is sufficient for cooking it; hence, let them be measured [well] before they are served out!'

Now (as regards a king's daily course of life), a king, on rising, when he has scarcely washed his mouth fully, must devote the first watch of the day to the examination of the day's receipts and expenditures, admitting (i.e. taking into account) a handful or half a handful (of anything); and yet even while he hears, the clever superintendents will defraud him of twice as much. By the force of their own ingenuity, they multiply a thousandfold the forty modes of defrauding set forth by Cāṇakya. In the second watch, the prince, with his ears painfully assailed by the squabbles of contending subjects, lives a most wretched life. Even there, the judges and others, disposing of the suits favourably or unfavourably to the litigants as they please, join their sovereign with sin and infamy—and, indeed, themselves with money! In the third watch, he finds leisure to bathe and eat; but, until his food is digested, he lives in dread of poison. In the fourth, he rises to stretch forth his hands to receive gold. In the fifth, he has to suffer great consternation on account of the anxiety of political schemes. In presenting these too, the counsellors, appearing to be neutral, enter into mutual agreement [i.e. conspire], and wilfully pervert merits and defects, misstate the reports of the ambassadors and spies, misrepresent possibilities and impossibilities, confound all distinctions of place and time, and prey upon the friends of their own partisans or enemies; and, secretly stirring up internal and external factions and openly appearing to subdue these, they bring their helpless master into their power. In the sixth, the king is [allowed] to divert himself as he likes, or to consult with his ministers—and the time thus allotted for amusement is [only] an hour and a half! In the seventh watch, he has the troublesome task of reviewing his troops. In the eighth, he has to worry himself with ambitious projects in the company of his generals. In the first watch of the night, after the performance of the twilight duties, he must receive his secret emmissaries, and through them instruct their cruel agents given the work of using swords, arson, or poison. After eating, he must, in the second watch of the night, begin to memorize his lessons like a Brāhmaṇa. In the night's third watch, he is sent to sleep with the sound of trumpets; a sleep he may be allowed to enjoy through the fourth and fifth watches—but how may the poor fellow find rest, with his mind distracted by constant anxieties? In the sixth watch, he must begin to prepare [to perform] the duties imposed upon him by the *sāstras,* as well as [other] business to be attended to. In the seventh watch, he must consult with ministers regarding the dispatch of agents and emissaries; and these fellows, as is well-known, say sweet things in order to increase the money [they take] from both sides, by trading on the road, being free from the fear of taxation; and making work, even in a slight degree, where there is none, wandering about freely. In the eighth watch the *Purohita* [priests] and others, assembling, tell the king—'Last night we saw an inauspicious dream;

the planets are inauspiciously arrayed; besides, there are evil portents. So let propitiatory rites be performed! Let all the sacrificial implements be made of gold; when this is done, the rites will be prolificly successful. Here are these Brāhmaṇas each like Brahmā himself. The benedictory rites performed by these lead to blissful results. They are in dreadful poverty; have large families [to support]; are constantly engaged in devotional rituals; are endowed with Brāhmaṇical lustre; and yet [still] have not received any donations from you. Whatever is given to them will be rewarded by a long life, heaven-like happiness, and the destruction of calamities.' And, thus having persuaded the king to confer rich donations, they secretly make themselves rich. Thus the troublesome, worrisome day and night are spent without happiness. The prince ruled by political advisors will find it difficult to preserve his sovereignty; the kingdom will find it difficult to persevere at all! There is a general mistrust regarding whatever a politician's prince gives, esteems or speaks of fondly: all that will be dismissed as intended to deceive. And mistrust is the cause of disaster. The extent to which the course of worldly existence can proceed without [artificial] policy may be observed from the experience of everyday life. We need have no recourse to *śāstras* in this business; even the suckling child manages to get milk from his mother. Then abandon all restraint and enjoy sense-pleasures as much as you can. Even those who advise you, 'the senses should be subdued'; 'the six natural enemies should be shunned'; 'one should pacify allies as well as friends'; and, 'all one's time should be spent in discussing questions of war and peace, with no time wasted in seeking pleasure'—the same hypocritical counsellors take whatever money they manage to pilfer from you and spend it in whorehouses. What about these beggars? Take the case of such stern dictators of policy as Śukra, Aṅgiras, Viśāla, Akṣabāhu, Dantīputra, Parāśara and the rest of the preceptors of *śāstras* and practical government. Did they subdue the six enemies? Did they put the precepts of the *śāstras* into practice? They too met with success and failure in their undertakings.[31]

In assessing Daṇḍin's achievements in the areas of satire and social criticism, it should be noted that the entire *Daśakumāracarita* contains a balanced view which is not obvious in the passages referred to above, which were selected with the intention of underscoring Daṇḍin's critical treatment of superstitions, Brāhmaṇic abuses, ascetics' weaknesses and state corruption. For example, while no one would deny the probable accuracy of Vihārabhadra's delineation of the means Brāhmaṇa advisors might employ to subject a king into haplessly aiding them in the pursuit of their own self-serving ends, it should also be pointed out that the king who follows this advice to enjoy sense-pleasures to the neglect of the study of statecraft is ultimately shorn of both kingdom and life through the machinations of a foreign agent who engineers a calamitous defeat after first weakening that king, his army and whole society by further promoting the mindless pursuit of fleeting pleasures. When the king is defeated, Daṇḍin simply explains that the loss was due to an insufficient training in polity. And while, on the one hand, Daṇḍin narrates a hilarious catalogue of the sexual aberrations of the Hindu gods and *ṛṣis* in the discourse of Kāmamañjarī, he also, on the other hand, leaves little doubt that the sage Marīci commits a pathetic blunder in accepting her arguments that *dharma* is unsullied by an occasional misadventure in the realm of *kāma*. Indeed, in the tale of Kāmamañjarī's next victim, we are given an affirmation of faith in the gods of the *paurāṇika* Hindu trinity. The victim was a scion of a wealthy Brāhmaṇa family, who, though lacking physical attractiveness, engaged a handsome though penniless youth in a contest for Kāmamañjarī's affections. Winning the contest, he lost his fortune to the extent of becoming reduced to the ownership of a single loin-cloth. In his despair, he cast aside the loin-cloth too, and took initiation as a 'sky-clad' Jaina monk. But, as is the custom in the rigorously austere career of Jaina monks, his hair and beard have been painfully plucked out by the roots, his body has been caked with dirt and wrecked by hunger and thirst. He fears damnation through hearing blasphemies concerning Brahmā, Viṣṇu and Śiva. Having retired to an Aśoka grove, he weeps piteously and recants his heresy. We have seen, however, in the *Daśakumāracarita* little of the idealization of Brāhmaṇas which is so characteristic of Kālidāsa. When Daṇḍin refers to them as 'the gods living on this earth', the context reveals the epithet to be sarcastic.

Daṇḍin's Brāhmaṇas are very worldly indeed: we have already seen mention of Brāhmaṇas' predilections for bordellos; and one of the few Brāhmaṇas who apparently meets with Daṇḍin's approval is the character Pramati, who chews betel, attends cockfights and insinuates himself into the royal harem by adopting women's clothes.[32]

Social Criticism and Caricature in Bāṇa's Kādambarī

The *Daśakumāracarita* contains several stylistic *tours de force*; notably, an entire chapter narrated without the use of labial letters, supposedly by a character with a sore lip. In another work often attributed to Daṇḍin, a treatise on poetics named the *Kāvyādarśa*, the author commends the copious use of compounds (*samāsabhūyastvam*). Stylistic pyrotechniques and profusion of compounds find their zenith in another romance of the seventh century, the *Kādambarī* of Bāṇa. The *Kādambarī* lacks the picaresque realism of the *Daśakumāracarita*; in the *Kādambarī* the satiric naturalism of the *Daśakumāracarita* is replaced by romantic fantasy. Yet, there are two sections in the *Kādambarī* which suggest social criticism.

The first place where we find something akin to social criticism is the advice of the aged counsellor, Śukanāsa, to the young hero, Candrāpīḍa, in a section known as the *Śukanāsopadeśa.* The sententious *upadeśa* imparted centres mainly on the defects of wealth and the corrupting influence of kingly power.

At first glance, it is both mildly shocking and humorous to see the personification of wealth and fortune, the Hindu goddess Lakṣmī, denounced by Śukanāsa as a whore who flits from man to man with no regard for virtue, learning, upbringing or generosity. Like lightning, she produces a short-lived flash and is gone. Like a dreadful *piśācī*, she intimidates men. As if jealous, she refuses to embrace a man favoured by Sarasvatī (the goddess of learning). As if fearful of ritual pollution, she refuses to touch a virtuous man. She drives a noble-minded man from her thoughts, as if he were inauspicious. She will not look upon a good man, as if he were an evil omen. She steps over a high-born man, as if he were a snake. She steps around a brave man, as if he were a thorn in her path. She forgets a generous man, as if he were a bad dream. She avoids an educated man, as if he were a villain. She taunts a noble person, as if he were a drunkard.

Though attached to the best of men (*puruṣottama*—Viṣṇu), still she loves the wicked. She acts as a cataract to the eyes of the *śāstras*; as a club in driving away good advice; as the slaughter-house of good intentions.

As for the corrupting influence of power affecting kings, Śukanāsa compares its actions to elements in the king's consecration ceremony. It is as though a king's courtesy were washed away by the sacred waters; as though his heart were darkened by the smoke of the sacred fire; as though his forgiveness were swept away by the sacred *kuśa* grass; as though his regard for heaven were obscured by the royal parasol; and, as though the good advice offered him were drained out by the cheers of the multitude. Like men about to die, kings fail to recognize their kinsmen; like the myopic, they lose their foresight; like the haunted, their houses become filled with vile creatures.

The self-serving counsellors of kings fare no better. They are compared to vultures feasting upon the flesh of wealth. They make it their business to misrepresent vices as virtues; laxity as beneficent administration; the passive witnessing of atrocities as profundity; the accolades of sycophantic poets as authentic fame; and indecision as impartiality.[33]

Only one other short sketch in the *Kādambarī* features satirical elements. Strictly speaking, the sketch might best be described as a literary caricature of an irrascible old Southern ascetic (*jaraddrāviḍadhārmikavarṇanam*). The hero of the romance, Candrāpīḍa, encounters the *drāviḍadhārmika* at a dilapidated Durgā shrine where the prince rests his horses during his return to his father's capital. The fact that the satirical description of the ascetic whom Candrāpīḍa finds there plays no role in the plot of the romance leads one to conclude that Bāṇa merely intended a caricature of the type of individual his audience would enjoy seeing lampooned. If the caricature is somewhat gratuitous, it is still worth mention in this essay becauseB āṇa digresses here in order to criticize a type which we shall often see satirized in later literature: namely, the Śaiva ascetic who renounces the world in order to better succeed in his attempts to manipulate it.

In his description of the old Śaiva ascetic, Bāṇa employs his considerable descriptive talents in an exhaustive catalogue of the character's physical deformities and ailments. While this detailed depiction of bodily imperfections may strike the reader as a particularly mean species of humour, it is worth noting that in Indian literature, as in Western literature, satirists (Kṣemendra, for example) have had recourse to this device as a means of providing the reader with concrete indices to the mental abnormalities of the character so depicted. So, the gullibility of the ascetic is indicated by his one eye destroyed by the magic ointment given to him by a charlatan; and his vanity is indicated by the darkening of the other eye due to his application of collyrium thrice daily. He suffers from a fever induced by his use of quack remedies. His back has been repeatedly injured in his inhospitable attempts to drive away wayfarers intent on spending the night at the shrine. He has tortured his body in his rage at the respect shown by the local populace to other ascetics passing through the area.

It is clear that the renunciation of this misfit stemmed not from dispassion with regard to the world, but rather as a compromise made in order to advance his aggrandizement of personal powers at the expense of others. Thus, his prayers to Durgā have not stemmed from devotion (*bhakti*), but rather in the preposterous hope that he might be conferred the rulership of the South as a boon. Instead of rejecting materialism, he has put his hopes on the manufacture of a magical wealth-conferring *tilaka* mark he learned of from a *śramaṇa* charlatan. He is obsessed with the notion of finding a treasure-trove, and with wild accounts of a Śrīśaila or 'mountain of wealth'. He is also obsessed with alchemists' depictions of the acquisition of instant wealth and has collected manuscripts full of spells, mystical formulae and *mantras* in the hope of furthering his materialistic ambitions by magical means. Nor has age and infirmity quelled his lechery: we learn that whatever celibacy he has practised has been through necessity rather than by choice.[34] He clings to the delusion that his *mantras* will secure him a *yakṣiṇī* lover. He has used a supposedly magic powder in the hope of compelling the submission of an old female ascetic.[35]

The passages referred to above reveal Bāṇa to be a writer capable of giving full vent to criticism of the faults of wealth, corrupt kings and flawed ascetics. Yet the extremely recondite allusions and paranomasias and extraordinarily lengthy compounds which characterize his style leave no doubt that he composed for a select audience of the very learned at court. That he was successful in finding such an audience is attested by several references to his winning of great fame through his *kāvyas.*[36]

Bhartṛhari

Turning to another author who, like Bāṇa, most probably lived the courtly life in seventh century India, we find more social criticism expressed in an easier, more popular style in the three centuries of verses ascribed to Bhartṛhari. Popular tradition has it that Bhartṛhari was a king saddened by his wife's infidelity and frustrated in his own attempts to find love outside of marriage, and who subsequently hovered between a fascination with the allurements of worldly life and the renunciation of a monk. Verses in the collection ascribed to him are cited as proof of this conjecture. The first verse is as follows:

Yāṃ cintayāmi satatam mayi sā viraktā
Sāpyanyamicchati janaṃ sa jano'nysaktaḥ /
Asmatkṛte ca pariśuṣyati kācidanyā
Dhiktāṃ ca taṃ ca madanaṃ ca imāṃ ca māṃ ca //[37]
The one I ponder is disinclined towards me;
She wants a man attached to yet another /
Another woman, withers for my sake:
Damn her! Damn him! Damn Kāma! Damn the other woman! Damn me! //

Another verse mirrors the tension in the poet's mind between sensuality and religion:

Keśāḥ saṃyaminaḥ śruterapi param pāraṃ gate locane
Antarvaktramapi svabhāvaśucibhiḥ kīrṇaṃ dvijānāṃ gaṇaiḥ /
Muktānāṃ satatādhivāsaruciraṃ vakṣojakumbhadvayam
Itthaṃ tanvi! vapuḥ praśāntamapi te kṣobhaṃ karotyeva naḥ //[38]
Hair tied in a braid, and eyes stretching to the ears,
A mouth filled with pure white teeth, /
Breasts pleasing through their constant adornment by pearls
O girl! Thus, your body is at rest—still, it disturbs me! //

The full sense of this verse can only be gathered with attention to the poetic suggestions *(dhvanis)* implicit in it. The phrase translated as 'hair tied in a braid', suggests 'restraining the senses' a reference to the matted hair of ascetics. 'Eyes stretching to the ears' suggests 'eyes taking in the supreme goal of the sacred literature'. 'A mouth filled with pure white teeth' suggests '(Brahmā's) mouth[39] filled with Brāhmaṇas pure by nature'. 'Pleasing through their constant adornment by pearls' suggests 'pleasing through the constant association with liberated souls'. Thus the beloved's body suggests the serenity of religion, yet it disturbs the poet! The tension between sensuality and religious motive is perfectly expressed in this verse by the device known as *virodhābhāsa*,[40] in which an apparent paradox is resolved by taking into account the suggested secondary meanings of the paronomasias.[41]

This last verse is accepted as a genuine member of the authentic Bhartṛhari collection assembled in D. D. Kosambi's critical edition. But the first verse is included among verses whose attribution to Bhartṛhari is doubtful. Even if the verse were authentic, there is nothing in it to suggest that the poet Bhartṛhari was a king. Although many of Bhartṛhari's verses reveal an insider's view of life at court, their tenor suggests the complaints of a learned courtier frustrated with the stupidity of kings and the groveling sycophants surrounding them. These verses will now be considered for social criticism which they voice.

It becomes even more difficult to believe that Bhartṛhari was ever a king when one reads the following verse in which Bhartṛhari compares a king's statecraft to a whore:

Satyānṛtā ca paruṣā priyavādinī ca
Hiṃsrā dayālurapi cārthaparā vadānyā /
Nityavyayā pracuranityadhanāgamā ca
Vārāṅganeva nṛpanītiranekarupā //[42]
Both true and false, both harsh and sweetly spoken,
Vicious and compassionate both, miserly and generous,
With both constant expenditure and constant copious income,
A king's polity, like a whore, has many faces.

A pair of verses voice criticism of the ill behaviour of kings toward the wise. The first speaks of men of learning undervalued in the realms of philistine kings:

Śāstropaskṛtaśabdasundaragiraḥ śiṣyapradeyāgamā
Vikhyātāḥ kavayao vasanti viṣaye yasya prabhor nirdhanāḥ |
Tajjāḍyaṃ vasudhādhipasya sudhiyo hyarthaṃ vināpīśvarāḥ
Kutsyāḥ syuḥ kuparīkṣakair na maṇayo yairarghataḥ pātitāḥ ||[43]

Their speech pleasing because of correct grammar and adorned with [allusions to] learned texts,
Their traditions deserving transmission to students—
In a kingdom where [such] celebrated sages dwell penniless,
This [only shows] the obtuseness of the king—the wise are wealthy without money.
Let those who apply worthless tests be condemned, not the jewels they devalue!

The next verse calls upon kings to renounce their arrogance towards the learned:

hartur yāti na gocaraṃ kimapi śam puṣṇāti yat sarvadā
arthibhyaḥ pratipādyamānamaniśaṃ prāpnoti vṛddhiṃ parām |
kalpānteṣvapi na prayāti nidhanaṃ vidyākhyam antardhanam
yeṣāṃ tān prati mānamujjhata nṛpāḥ kastaiḥ saha spardhate || [44]

It does not fall prey to a thief; it always promotes a kind of peace;
Imparted to its seekers, it never fails to grow;
It is not lost even at the end of time: such is the inner treasure called knowledge.
O kings, give up your arrogance towards its possessors! Who can contend with them?

The next group of verses is on the theme of the pitfalls inherent in the service of the rich and powerful. The first speaks knowingly of the difficulties faced by servants or, perhaps, courtiers with regard to the slanders to which they are subjected by hostile critics:

maunān-mūkaḥ pravacanapaṭur vātalo jalpako vā
dhṛṣṭaḥ pārśve bhavati ca tathā dūrato'pyapragalbhaḥ |
kṣāntyā bhīrur-yadi na sahate prāyaśo nābhijātaḥ
sevādharmaḥ paramagahano yogīnām-apyagamayaḥ ||[45]

If silent, a 'dummy';

If eloquent, 'prolix' or a 'senseless babbler';
If intimate, 'importunate',
Or 'immature', if distant;
By forebearance, 'timid';
Or, 'ill-bred' if not complacent:
The nature of service is utterly impenetrable,
Eluding even the wise.

The following *śloka* laments the ascription of all virtues to those who have money:[46]

yasyāsti vittaṃ sa naraḥ kulīnaḥ
sa paṇḍitaḥ sa śrutavān guṇajñaḥ /
sa eva vaktā sa ca darśanīyaḥ
sarve guṇāḥ kāñcanam āśrayanti //[47]
A monied man is thought well-born,
Wise, learned and a judge of virtue.
He alone is thought eloquent, even handsome:
All virtues attend upon gold!

The sycophant is devastatingly compared to a groveling dog, while his opposite is compared to a lordly elephant in a pair of *dṛṣṭāntas*:[48]

lāṅgūlaālanam adhaścaraṇāvapātaṃ
bhūmau nipatya vadanodaradarśanaṃ ca /
śvā piṇḍadasya kurute gajapuṃgavas-tu
dhīraṃ vilokayati cāṭuśataiś-ca bhuṅkte //[49]
A dog falls on the ground before the donor of a scrap,
Wags his tail, rolls at his master's feet, and displays his mouth and belly.
But a lordly elephant looks on impassively
And eats only after hundreds of cajoleries.

The verse which follows is fatalistic in its view of the acquisition of wealth, and admonishes its reader not to grovel before the rich:

yad dhātrā nijabhālapaṭṭalikhitaṃ stokam mahad vā dhanaṃ
tat prāpnoti marusthale'pi nitarām merau ca nāto'dhikam /

tad dhīro bhava vittavatsu kṛpaṇāṃ vṛttiṃ vṛthā mā kṛtāḥ
kūpe paśya payonidhāv api ghaṭo gṛhṇāti tulyaṃ jalam //[50]

Whatever wealth, great or little, the Creator has inscribed on one's forehead,
So much will one unquestionably obtain, even in a wasteland —but no more, even on the mountain of gold!
Therefore, be resolute and do not uselessly play the toady before the rich!
See, the pot takes the same amount of water from the ocean or a well!

Although there will be occasion to refer again to Bhartṛhari in subsequent chapters, the above verse provides a convenient transition to the *Pañcatantra*'s critical realism with respect to wealth and poverty.

The Pañcatantra *on Privilege, Poverty and Servitude*

Throughout the Nīti literature, the very profusion of sympathetic portrayals of the miseries of poverty is in itself sufficient to demonstrate a significant degree of social conscience in Sanskrit. Even D. D. Kosambi concedes that poverty 'seems to be the only reality with which the poet of the classical period came to grips', but he immediately stipulates that the only poverty which concerned such a poet was the poverty of his own class.[51] It seems to me impossible to prove that all or even a majority of complaints against poverty in Sanskrit springs from poets' selfish class interests or demonstrate their inability to generalize from their own experience of deprivation—assuming, for the sake of argument, that such was their plight—to that of others. Certainly verses from the *Pañcatantra* do much to suggest sympathy rather than selfishness.

Wealth, according to the *Pañcatantra*,[52] confers unfair advantage upon its possessors while the poor suffer a consequent lack of opportunity. If a man is observed to be ever cocksure, speaking arrogantly and domineering, then we may be sure his strength comes from money (2.89). But,

śūraḥ surūpaḥ subhagaśca vāgmī
śastrāṇi śāstrāṇi vidāṅkarotu /

> *arthaṃ vinā naiva yaśaśca mānaṃ*
> *prāpnoti marttyo'tra manuṣyaloke* // (5.25)
> Should an ordinary mortal be brave, handsome, amiable, eloquent and learned with respect to both weapons and texts; nevertheless, without money, he will gain neither fame nor respect in this human sphere.

The words *atra* and *manuṣyaloke* deserve special mention here. The poet who wrote the *Pañcatantra* pointedly reminds his readers frequently that he speaks of *this* world with all its imperfections and *not*, by implication, the earthly paradises dreamed up by the *mahākavis*. In their idealized world, virtue never fails to be rewarded and poverty is seldom even suggested. But here, in this world, as the *Pañcatantra*'s poet puts it,

> *vikalamiha pūrvasukṛtaṃ vidyāvanto'pi kulasamudbhūtāḥ* /
> *yasya yadā vibhavaḥ syāt tasya tadā dāsatāṃ yānti* //
> Previous good turns count for nought: in this world, even well-bred men of learning become the slaves of whomever has money at the time. (5.9)

Of course, it is not 'this world' literally which is responsible for this injustice, but rather the men who populate it and colour it with their philistine values:

> *sukulaṃ kuśalaṃ sujanaṃ vihāya kulakuśulaśīlavikale'pi* /
> *āḍhye kalpatarāviva nityaṃ rajyanti jananivahāḥ* //
> Turning away from a decent[53] man of talent and breeding, the mob becomes as fascinated with a rich man as if he were wishing-tree, though he lacks breeding, talent or character. (5.8)

In the eyes of the world then, virtues without money lose their lustre: 'Character, purity, forgiveness, skill, gentility and noble birth—all these fail utterly to lend lustre to an impoverished man' (5.2). The poet here and in the next two verses plays upon the convention within Sanskrit poetry which associates success with property of shiningness. Thus, the fame attendant upon success is itself considered fancifully to be white in colour (cf. the proper name, 'Candrakīrti', referring to one whose fame is like the moon in implied whiteness and luminosity). There is also in this imagery a connotation of the loss of self-confidence which, of course, goes well with the condition of being both impoverished and reduced to beg the indulgence of others. Thus Sanskrit poets describe the impoverished as *niṣpratibha*, literally, 'lacklustre', but perhaps better rendered as 'crestfallen' or even 'depressed' or 'downtrodden'. So it is that the *Pañcatantra*'s poet declares that a poor man's various virtues—however excellent—do not shine forth in the least; but, by its very nature, wealth makes all qualities shine, even as the sun illumines all manner of things (2.94). In similar imagery, a poor man is said to be 'sullied' by his poverty, which, in turn, leads him to a state of utter humiliation (2.104). Moreover, akin to the concept of losing one's lustre through impoverishment is the notion that through the same process, one becomes unsightly to the degree that, in accordance with commonplace Hindu superstitions, even to be observed is to expose your beholder to possible misfortune. Thus, a poor man is said to be avoided exactly like several tabooed objects (2.107). For all intents and purposes, the poor man is dead (2.101); even his own kinsmen look upon him as if he were dead (2.103). His kinsmen suffer embarrassment on his account and seek to conceal their connection to him; similarly, his friends become estranged (2.105). And, if that were not enough, his master, though well-served, becomes hostile; his wife becomes insolent; his sons will abandon him (5.25). And still the burden of having a family continues: though he be of considerable intellect, still his mind is wasted on worry over butter, salt, oil, grain, clothing and fuel (5.4 and 5). His status is diminished to such a degree that he stands below ritually unclean, inanimate dirt: even clay left over from toilet routines finds some use, whereas the poor man is of no use to anyone (2.108). If he approaches someone with more money, the latter avoids him, suspecting him to have come to beg (2.109) or steal (2.97),[54] though in both cases the poor man may have only approached his more fortunate acquaintance with the intention of doing him a favour!

Perhaps more frustrating than being shunned is the poor man's experience of being totally ignored. Even with effort, no one will seemingly be able to see him, the gloom of his poverty obscures him even on a sunlit day (2.99). His existence is in name only (2.91 and 93). Any fate is preferable to that of living off kinsmen (5.23) or begging (2.96). The poor are impotent (2.97); or, like widows of good breeding, their only alternative is to torture their minds with unfulfilled hopes (2.102); such hopes, again, are as useless as widows' breasts (2.98).

Moreover, if dependence on charity is unthinkable, its alternative, a life of servitude, is tantamount to living death (1.288), for servants are so intimidated that they are too nervous to eat freely, or to sleep soundly, or to speak without fear (1.289). A king's servants may feel their very lives insecure (1.285).

The *Pañcatantra* goes on to say even more about the miseries and injustices of poverty, yet I think that the references summarized above are sufficient to show undeniable sympathy for the poor and even outrage at their oppression—all this in marked contrast to the supercilious indifference one should expect to find in poetry of the court and of the privileged priestly class. The most significant feature of these many verses, however, is how very few in number they appear to be when contrasted with a myriad similar verses in the *subhāṣitasaṅgrahas*.

Criticism of Religious Hypocrisy Couched in Animal Fables

It is true that Brāhmaṇas are sometimes portrayed in the *Pañcatantra* and the *Hitopadeśa* in something less than the most flattering terms. Surely the reader is not expected to admire or emulate the sagacity of the Brāhmaṇa swindled out of his sacrificial goat in the *Hitopadeśa*. That hapless fellow rids himself of his goat after becoming persuaded that it is a dog, the touch of which, no doubt, is ritually polluting. Other Brāhmaṇas are depicted as crafty or lazy, spurred into action only by shrewish wives; yet, A. B. Keith rightly notes[55] that such irreverence does not constitute a sweeping condemnation of Brāhmaṇas as a class. This kind of distinction is one to which we shall have recourse several times in subsequent discussion of Hindu criticism of its religious; whole sub-classes may be found objectionable, yet a suggestion is usually present to the effect that the counterfeit religious would not, *could* not succeed in their perfidy were it not for the acknowledged existence of the genuinely religious.

Having said that, I must admit that more than moderate criticism is intended in the following verse:

> *narakāya matis te cet paurohityaṃ samācara |*
> *varṣaṃ yāvat kimanyena maṭhacintāṃ dinatrayam ||*
> If your mind is set on going to hell, then just serve a year as a (*purohita*) priest; or, if time is short, spend but three days overseeing a *maṭha*![56] (2.70)

Similarly, there is clearly something short of fawning obeisance in the naming of two wandering monks (*parivrājakas*) as 'Tāmracūḍa' or 'Bald as a Copper Pot' and 'Bṛhatsphic'—'Big Ass'.[57] Yet, apart from these isolated barbs, the most consistent theme of criticism of the religious in these texts involves vignettes in which villainous animals sham sanctity in order to better promote their nefarious exploitation of the gullible.

The stories of the *Pañcatantra* and the *Hitopadeśa* in which beasts sham asceticism have antecedents in the *Mahābhārata* and the *Jātaka* collections. The *Mahābhārata* tells the story of a cat on the bank of the Gaṅgā (Ganges) who counterfeits asceticism by holding aloft his paw (being *ūrdhvabāhu*) with the motive of devouring impressionable birds and mice (5.160.15-43). This hypocrite finds parallel representations in the *Biḷāra Jātaka* (128), the *Pañcatantra* (3.2) and the *Hitopadeśa* (1.4).[58] An interesting feature of *Hitopadeśa* tale is that the hypocritical cat ascetic must first insinuate himself into the confidence of an old and blind guardian of infant birds. This he accomplishes through the pretense of having come to learn *dharma* from the blind watchbird, who cannot resist the opportunity to share his expertise in this subject.

In several of these tales, an animal finds himself quite by accident endowed with a mark of sainthood and the impetus which this event provides to his latent treachery proves to be an irresistible temptation. So it is in several *Jātaka* tales and also in the *Pañcatantra* (p. 140 of Hertel's edition), where a cat becomes adorned with a monk's necklace through the accident of having gotten his head stuck in a butter pot. And so it is too with the *Hitopadeśa*'s celebrated jackal who falls into a vat of indigo dye and subsequently utilizes this fortuitous circumstance—his new colour is the same as Viṣṇu's *avatāras*—to tyrannize the awed beasts of the forest.

Occasionally the beasts of these stories adopt the confidence man's trick of appealing to something within his victim's baser nature in order to gain his object. We have seen above how an old and blind vulture could not resist being sought as an authority on *dharma*. In the *Hitopadeśa* (1.3), a tiger feeds himself upon victims through dangling the prospect of a gold bracelet before them—all the while explaining that, in his personal saintliness, he has renounced all attachment for such material objects. Providing an easy objective correlative to the attachment which the tiger piques in his victims' minds, the *Hitopadeśa* portrays one such greedy fellow becoming caught in a mire where he is subsequently devoured by his no longer saintly guide. This victim would have done well to heed the words of the *Pañcatantra*:

> *ekākī gṛhasantyaktaḥ pāṇipātro digambaraḥ |*
> *so'pi saṃvāhyate loke tṛṣṇayā paśya kautukam ||*
> Behold something extraordinary! In this world, even the most aloof Digambara (naked) ascetic—who has renounced his home forever and uses nothing more than his own hands as a begging bowl—is still swept away by desire! (5.5 in the Calcutta edition).

In concluding this chapter, I hope it is apparent from all the examples presented above that social conscience and social criticism are well represented even within some of the most often read works of Sanskrit literature. In almost every case, more examples could be added to those given above; yet, I hope that the reader will agree with me that such addition would be superfluous. Even the animal fables of the *Pañcatantra* and the *Hitopadeśa* offer further criticism of religious counterfeits; yet, at this point, it would seem more profitable to shift to a new author's utilization of the same themes. We will next see how Kṣemendra begins with imagery borrowed from the animal fables and continues to form satire through his own style.

References

1. G.R. Nandargikar, *The Raghuvaṃśa of Kālidāsa*, Poona, 1897, p. 201.
2. *HSL*, p. 82.
3. Kālidāsa repeats the condemnation of the *Rāmāyaṇa* in the instance of a Śūdra who dares to cross caste lines and engage himself in ascetic practices (*tapasyā*).
4. S.K. De, 'Wit, Humour. . .,' op. cit., p. 163.
5. Cf. Daniel H.H. Ingalls, 'Kālidāsa and the Attitudes of the Golden Age', *JAOS*, vol. 96, No. 1, Jan.–March 1976, pp. 15-26.
6. The profession of commerce was so forbidden to Brāhmaṇas that the *Baudhāyana Dharma Sūtra* orders that Brāhmaṇas who do engage in trade should be treated like Śūdras (I.5.10.24). Cf. Crawford, op. cit., pp. 89-90.
7. Cf. M.R. Kale, *The Mṛcchakaṭika of Śūdraka*, p. 157 of the Notes, where Kale draws upon the *Yājñavalkya Smṛti* for illustrations of the ordeals mentioned by Cārudatta at the close of the Ninth Act.
8. The scholar was Pischel; cf. Keith, *HSL*, p. 296.
9. Cf. M.H. Abrams, *A Glossary of Literary Terms*, p. 59.
10. T.V. Mahalingam, *Kāñcīpuram in Early South Indian History*, pp. 120-21.
11. Cf. *The Daśakumāracarita of Daṇḍin*, ed. M.R. Kale, pp. 178–80.
12. D.K. Gupta, *Society and Culture in the Time of Daṇḍin*, pp. 341–43.
13. The *Daśakumāracarita*, pp. 166–70 of Kale's edition.
14. The sorcerer is termed as a '*narendra*' which, in his commentary, Kale glosses as '*mantrajña*'. Cf. the commentary on p. 172 of Kale's edition of the Sanskrit text.
15. The 'magicians' are again '*narendras*', which Kale glosses as '*mantravādins*.' Cf. p. 178 of his edition of the Sanskrit text.
16. The *Pūrvapīṭhikā* and *Uttarapīṭhikā* sections of the work are generally thought to be the work of later interpolators. Cf. Keith, *HSL*, pp. 298-99 and below n. 32.
17. Duties, her mother notes, imposed upon the prostitute by no less a personage than the creator-god, Brahmā himself!
18. Tilottamā was an *apsarā* created by Viśvakarmā at Brahmā's command. The intention was to create dissention among the demons. It is possible that here Daṇḍin alludes to a lost recension of the *Mahābhārata*, for the story which comes down to us today in the *Ādiparvan* tells us that Brahmā and the *ṛṣis* were alone successful in withstanding Tilottamā's charm. As the circumambulated the celestials, three new faces appeared on Śiva, and Indrá developed a thousand eyes. Cf. Sorensen's *Index to Names in the Mahābhārata*, under 'Tilottamā', p. 676 (citing *Mbh*. I.208).
19. 'It is said that Śiva once visited a forest in the form of a religious mendicant, and the wives of the *ṛṣis* residing there fell in love with his great beauty, which the *ṛṣis*, perceiving, resented; in order, therefore, to overpower him, they first dug a pit, and by magical arts caused a tiger to rush out of it, whom he [Śiva] slew, and taking his skin wore it as a garment.' Dowson quoted by M.R. Kale on p. 46 of his notes. In *Hindu Polytheism* (p. 216), A. Danielou quotes Dowson's account verbatim without crediting him.

20. Cf. the *Bhāgavata Purāṇa* (Gītā Press edn.), X.59.33, where the number is put at 16,100 after a reading of the *Viṣṇu Purāṇa* (V. 39.9 and 31). Cf. also the Gītā Press edn. of the *Bhāgavata Purāṇa*, X.69.8 and 44. The classic account is in the *Bhāgavata Purāṇa*, X.29–34.

21. The daughter was Sarasvatī. She attempted to elude her lecherous father by transforming herself into a doe, but Brahmā assumed the form of a buck and continued the chase until his head was shorn by Śiva's arrow. The great Hindu apologist, Kumārila Bhaṭṭa, attempted to explain the myth away as an allegory of the sun following dawn. Cf. Kale's notes, p. 46.

22. The story appears with variations in the *Mahābhārata* (cf. Sorensen's *Index*, p. 24, citing *Mbh*. V.12.373), the *Rāmāyaṇa* (cf. I.48.15–30 of the Gujarati Press edn.), and in the *Kathāsaritsāgara* (cf. the Delhi edn. of the Sanskrit text, III.3.136–47, p. 59).

23. After performing the Rājasūya sacrifice, Soma (the moon) grew intoxicated with pride and ravished Bṛhaspati's wife Tārā. Urged repeatedly by Bṛhaspati, neither Brahmā nor the *devarṣis* could induce Soma to release Tārā. Aṅgirasa, Śiva and Indra came to Bṛhaspati's aid, and, after a considerable battle involving gods and the *dānavas*, Brahmā was at length successful in restoring Tārā to Bṛhaspati. The union of Tārā and Soma was instrumental to the founding of the lunar dynasty. The story is taken from the *Viṣṇu Purāṇa* (Gita Press edn. of the text, pp. 310–12) IV.6.8–33.

24. The union resulting in the celebrated twin physicians of the gods, the śvins. Cf. Sorensen's *Index*, p. 11, citing *Mbh*. I.66.

25. Añjanā resisted Vāyu's advances in the interest of preserving her chastity and so conceived Hanumān, without intercourse. The tale provides an intriguing parallel to myths of parthenogenesis in a variety of other cultures.

26. An interesting story accounting for the scandalous births of two revered Vedic *ṛṣis*, Bharadvāja and Dīrghatamas. After first impregnating his elder brother's wife with the foetus of Bharadvāja, Bṛhaspati approached her again while she was still carrying a second child. Even the child protested against Bṛhaspati's unseemly advances, with the result that Bṛhaspati cursed the child to remain in everlasting darkness; hence the name Dīrghatamas. Cf. Sorensen's *Index*, p. 255. Sorensen puts the story in the *Bhīṣma-satyavatī-saṃvāda* section; I found it in the following chapter of the Poona edn. (the older one, with Nīlakaṇṭha's commentary) I.104.10–22; I.98.7–16 in the Critical Edition. The effectiveness of the example to Kāmamañjarī's argument will be noted when it is recalled that Bṛhaspati is the venerable *guru* of the gods.

27. The fisherman's daughter's low caste and childhood should be noted in this story. In the text Daṇḍin refers to the girl's '*dūṣaṇam*' by Parāśara, a word which connotes 'deflowering' or 'despoiling'; this is somewhat at variance to the version in the *Mahābhārata* where the girl, like Añjanā above, conceives the child (Vyāsa) through parthenogenesis. Cf. Sorensen, p. 630, citing *Mbh*. I.63. Along the lines of Max-Müller, one would suspect a little sanctimonious editing of these *Mahābhārata* tales at a time somewhat later than Daṇḍin's.

28. Cf. Sorensen, loc. cit., citing *Mbh*. I.110. Vyāsa's impregnating the two wives of Vicitravīrya, Ambikā and Ambālikā, is alluded to here.

29. There were some extenuating circumstances: the wicked king had imprisoned Upahāravarman's parents and was an oppressive ruler.

30. This is a reference to the preparations for a *dikṣā* or initiation preparatory to a king's consecration.

31. This translation generally follows, with numerous exceptions, that of M.R. Kale, given on pp. 134–38 of the English section of his edition of the *Daśakumāracarita*.

32. Daṇḍin's treatment of Brāhmaṇas is in such contrast to that of the author of the *Pūrvapīṭhikā* that it forms one of the most convincing arguments for the rejection of the *Pūrvapīṭhikā* as a spurious interpolation. Cf. A.B. Keith:

> [The realism of Daṇḍin's outlook] stands out the more prominently when it is compared with the pious attitude of the author of the *Pūrvapīṭhikā*. To him the sacrifice is the power that brings the gods; Rājahaṃsa is praised because of his devotion to the priests, the gods on earth, while Daṇḍin denies them that appellation save in one passage where his use for them of *dharaṇītala-taitila* is sneering, the term meaning 'rhinoceroses.' The king's domestic priest possesses the full holiness of Brāhmaṇa himself, and despite his appalling deeds the Brāhmaṇa Mataṅga, because he died in saving another Brāhmaṇa, after an interesting tour of inspection of Yama's hells is restored to life, and by his devotion to Śiva is rewarded with the aid of Rājavāhana to aid him to win an *asura* princess and lordship of the nether regions. Not valour but Śiva's club gives the king of Mālava victory over Rājahaṃsa. Daṇḍin makes a joke out of Mārkaṇḍeya's curse which condemns Suratamañjarī, whose pearl necklace fell on the ascetic when bathing, to become a silver chain. The *Pūrvapīṭhikā* parts Śāmba from his wife for two months because of the curse of a water-fowl. The princes are no longer free agents; the great Vāmadeva and his acolytes protect and guard the father and the princess; Rājavāhana can win his princess only by a Brāhamaṇa's aid. (*HSL*, pp. 301–2)

33. *Bāṇa's Kādambarī*, ed., M.R. Kale, from the 'Śukanāsopadeśa', pp. 170–78.

34. Bāṇa tells us that his celibacy has been a *turagabrahmacarya*, a reference, if I am correct, to the enforced celibacy of one year imposed upon the stallion prior to the inauguration of the celebrated Aśvamedha sacrifice.

35. *Bāṇa's Kādambarī*, ed. M.R. Kale, pp. 167–79 of the Sanskrit text.

36. One may find such references in Sanskrit commentaries on the *Kāvyaprakāśa* of Mammaṭa. The second *kārikā* of the work refers to the role of *kāvya* in conferring celebrity on its author. Mammaṭa himself cites the cases of Kālidāsa and others, saying *kālidāsānādīnāmiva yaśaḥ*. In perhaps the best of the many commentaries on the *Kāvyaprakāśa*. the late Vāmanācārya Jhalakīkar explains, '*ādipadāddaṇḍibhāravibāṇa*-[my underscoring] *govardhanādayo grāhyāḥ*.' Cf. Jhalakīkar's edn. of the *Kāvyaprakāśa*, p. 7.

37. Given as the second *śloka* in the *Nīti-śatakam* in *The Nīti and Vairāgya Śatakas of Bhartṛhari*, ed. M.R. Kale, p. 2 of the text.

38. Given as verse 12 in the 'Śṛṅgāra-śatakam' in the *Subhāṣitatriśatī*, edited by D.D. Kosambi and N.R. Acarya, p. 66.

39. The word for 'mouth' in the verse is *vaktram*, and the word for Brāhmaṇas is *dvijas*. As Brāhmaṇas are said to be born from the mouth of Brahmā in Manu and elsewhere, they are styled *vaktraja*. Cf. any Sanskrit dictionary.

40. Cf. Ramacandra Budhendra's *Sanskrit Commentary*, p. 67 of the Kosambi-Acarya edition.

41. Cf. Edwin Gerow, *A Glossary of Indian Figures of Speech*, pp. 268-69.

42. Number 38 in the *Nīti-śataka* of Kosambi's edition, p. 24.

43. Number 11 in the *Nīti-śataka* of Kosambi's edition, p. 9.

44. Number 12 in the *Nīti-śataka* of Kosambi's edition, p. 10.

45. Number 47 in the *Nīti-śataka* of Kosambi's edition, p. 28.

46. For antecedents of this theme even as ancient as the *Ṛgveda*, cf., S.K. De writing in *Our Heritage*, vol. III (1955) p. 158: 'Scattered throughout Vedic literature we have witty, but cynical remarks about wealth and woman. In the *Ṛgveda*, for instance, one poet observes that wealth in the form of cows makes even the lean man fat and the ugly handsome (IV.28.6) [this reference is faulty, but I was able to locate it at (VI.28.6) by looking up the word *kṛśa* ('lean') in Viśva Bandhu's *Grammatical Word Index to the Four Vedas*], and buys the affection of many a maiden.'

47. Number 32 in the *Nīti-śataka* of Kosambi's edition, p. 20.

48. Gerow defines a *dṛṣṭānta* as 'the adjunction of a second situation [here, that of the sycophant, for example] which bears upon the same point as the first [the groveling dog] and where the purpose is entirely one of illustration.' And adds, 'The relationship is here between two specific situations, and the purpose of *rapprochement* is clarification. That is why a rigorous parallelism of element and aspect is required.' Op. cit., p. 199.

49. Number 23 in the *Nīti-śataka* of Kosambi's edition, p. 16.

50. Number 40 in the *Nīti-śataka* of Kosambi's edition, p. 25.

51. Ibid., pp. xliii-xliv.

52. Although other editions of the *Pañcatantra* will be referred to in the next section, citations, unless stipulated to refer to other editions should be assumed to be keyed to that of Jivananda Vidyasagar & Sons, Calcutta, 1930.

53. '. . .though poor' is implied. Cf. the Vidyasagar commentary, p. 506 of that edition.

54. The suspicion of robbery is suggested in the Vidyasagar commentary, p. 252.

55. *HSL*, p. 249.

56. In the commentary provided by Jivananda Vidyasagara & Sons, it is explained that a *purohita*'s routine involves either cheating the public outright or prostituting one's rituals through a lust for money (p. 237 of their edition).

57. Pp. 234-35 of the text of the same edition.

58. In these and subsequent citations, I follow those given in M. Bloomfield's 'False Ascetics and Nuns in Hindu Fiction', *JAOS*, 44 (1924) pp. 202–42.

Chapter 3

THE CONTRIBUTION OF KASHMIR

The Historical Background of Kṣemendra's Satires

In the most recent study to emerge on the life and works of Kṣemendra,[1] Rajatbaran Dattaray expresses a view of his subject which may well leave Kṣemendra scholars dumbfounded: namely, that 'it is but evident [*sic*] that Kṣemendra held the Brāhmaṇa community in high esteem.'[2] Before passing on to a critical appraisal of this conclusion, it is necessary to delve into Kṣemendra lore for a moment in order to fairly present its context.

To begin with, the reader should be informed that Kṣemendra, although unique in several ways in the history of Sanskrit literature, enjoys the further distinction of being one of those rare Sanskrit writers about whom some reliable biographical information has survived. We know that he lived a long life in Kashmir, highlighted by an almost equally long literary career of a little more than 50 years, extending from approximately A.D. 1015 to about 1066. Modern Indians sometimes point with pride to the anonymity enshrouding many works of literary and (especially) visual arts in India, finding there a selfless dedication less common in the West. Kashmiri authors, thankfully, were not nearly so modest;[3] Kṣemendra and his son Somendra not only take credit for their own compositions, but also provide us with the names of their forefathers, up to and including Kṣemendra's great grandfather. Their pride was understandable: not only had the family amassed a considerable fortune, but Kṣemendra's father, Prakāśendra, had also achieved celebrity through his philanthropic gifts to the community of Brāhmaṇas. The fact that this charity of his father's is mentioned in Kṣemendra's colophons shows, according to Dattaray, apparent 'special interest in. . .one of his father's special virtues: Prakāśendra's devotion to Brāhmaṇas, whose blessing he is stated to have earned by his generous charities to them' [*punctuation added*].[4] It is on *this* basis that Dattaray finds it 'evident that Kṣemendra held the Brāhmaṇa community in high esteem.'

It seems to me that the reasoning behind this assertion may be challenged on several grounds. First, even if we were to ignore the history of Kashmir for the moment, it would strike me as obvious that a distinction might well be drawn between, on the one hand, filial admiration of a generous father and, on the other hand, esteem for those on the dole; yet it is only the former whom Kṣemendra praises here. Moreover, tradition of Kashmir holds that Kṣemendra, notwithstanding his father's philanthropy, succeeded to a vast fortune. Yet, there is nothing in Kṣemendra's nor in his son's colophons to suggest that it ever occurred to Kṣemendra to emulate his father's example. Even if we accept verbatim the florid hyperbole[5] in Kṣemendra's descriptions of Prakāśendra's charity and devotion at death to Śiva, there is no reason to assume that such fanaticism was passed from father to son. Moreover, if we *do* assume exaggeration in Kṣemendra's praise, we may seek explanation for his father's generosity in simple political expediency. This would be the second reason to suspect Dattaray's conclusion; but, to understand it fully, we must have recourse to the history of Kashmir and the place of Kṣemendra's family in it.

We should begin with the question of how it was that Kṣemendra's forefathers acquired their admittedly great fortune. Sylvain Lévi suggested that a possible cause might be found in the identification of Prakāśendra's father, Sindhu, with a scoundrel of the same name in the *Rājataraṅgiṇī* who emptied the royal treasury under the nominal reign of Abhimanyu and Queen Diḍḍā (A.D. 958-1003).[6] Dr. Suryakanta admits that this identification is, as he puts it, 'tempting', and that 'the chronology also supports this.'[7] Yet, both Indian critics reject this identification. Both point out that the *Rājataraṅgiṇī* mentions Mataṅga as a son of the notorious Sindhu and makes no mention of Prakāśendra. Without bothering with the strained speculation that Mataṅga could have been another name by which Prakāśendra was known to Kalhaṇa, it seems altogether possible to me that both were Sindhu's sons, the former receiving mention in the *Rājataraṅgiṇī* due to the fact that he also served as a royal treasurer; the same history makes no mention of Prakāśendra by name, and mentions Kṣemendra only as the author of his *own* chronicle of the kings of Kashmir, the *Nṛpāvali*—regrettably now lost. Suryakanta's strongest argument is that the *Rājataraṅgiṇī* declares Sindhu's father to have been the 'litter-carrier, Kuyya', whereas Kṣemendra's son gives the name 'Bhogendra'. Neither Suryakanta nor Dattaray seem to have considered the possibility that Kalhaṇa might have harboured some enmity towards the family of his rival historian, Kṣemendra—whose *Nṛpāvali* he dismisses as inaccurate—and that the description of Sindhu's father as the 'litter-carrier, Kuyya' might well have been of the nature of an unkind epithet. Both Indian critics make much of the contrast between the 'very black' terms in which Sindhu is portrayed in the *Rājataraṅgiṇī* and Kṣemendra's complimentary treatment of his grandfather. It seems to me plausible that this might be equally well explained by the same grudge which I suspect Kalhaṇa bore towards Kṣemendra's family, together with a modicum of familial pride on Kṣemendra's part, if not an understandable desire to counter rival versions of the circumstances under which his family became so wealthy.

If I have succeeded in showing that there is still no incontrovertible ground for rejecting Lévi's identification of the two Sindhus, then there is all the more reason to suspect that Prakāśendra's generosity towards the Brāhmaṇa community might well have been a matter of simple expediency: for the Brāhmaṇas formed a very powerful special interest group in the political life of eleventh-century Kashmir. Writing of Kalhaṇa's assessment of this group, M. A. Stein writes that then they were 'organized into corporations (*parṣad*) at all the more important shrines and pilgrimage places and [were] often possessed of great endowments. . .[and] played more than once an important part in the internal politics of the country. The solemn fasts or Prāyopaveśas to which they were apt to resort in critical circumstances, were evidently powerful means of coercion which weak rulers had reason to dread.'[8] Moreover, 'Kalhaṇa does not hide his contempt for this priestly class whose ignorance was equal to its arrogance, and bitterly condemns their baneful interference in affairs of state.'[9] If Kṣemendra's grandfather was the same Sindhu whom Kalhaṇa describes as having made himself rich by drawing upon the royal treasury, then accounts of his son's generosity might only reflect nothing more noble than an apparently successful tactic to hold the meddlesome Brāhmaṇas at bay, buying their cooperation. Moreover, it should be noted that this explanation does not stand or fall on the assumption of the identity of the two Sindhus: given the notoriously unstable political circumstances of eleventh-century Kashmir, anyone possessed of extraordinary wealth might well have been forced to adopt such an expedient.

Kṣemendra's Satire of the Hindu Priestly Class

The strongest argument against the notion that Kṣemendra held the Brāhmaṇas in esteem is to be found in the hardly moderate terms with which he satirized their foibles. Kṣemendra's satire strikes at a broad range of faults he perceived in his society. As mentioned in the Introduction, I cannot possibly hope to the full scope of his criticism in an essay of this length; to a lesser extent, the same limitations of space and time forbid a thorough treatment of even the few topics I have chosen to include here.[10] Nevertheless, it is hoped that the material presented here will be found sufficient to at least suggest the character of Kṣemendra's social criticism. Perhaps the simplest way of introducing the reader to Kṣemendra's criticisms of the Brāhmaṇical class would be to present a translation of a passage from his *Kalāvilāsa*, 'The Flashing Play of Cunning.'

The setting of the passage is the story of a rich merchant who places his all too ingenuous son under the tutelage of Sanskrit literature's perennial prince of cunning, Mūladeva.[11] Mūladeva commends to the boy the cultivation of hypocrisy—specifically, hypocrisy of the religious variety (*dambha*).[12]

> Listen, O Son, to the most deceitful essence of all cunning. When it is mastered, even fleeting riches take on permanency. (1.39)
>
> In the impenetrable forest of life, there is one fatal pitfall, covered over with leaves and grass, into which the foolish plunge like guileless antelopes. (1.40)
>
> In this world there is one intrinsically profound treasure-trove, its mouth covered over with crooked snakes [called] cheats. It is called religious hypocrisy. (1.41)

Religious hypocrisy is the secret incantation (*mantra*) [which summons] deception; the magic wishing-jewel of those who crave riches; that through which scoundrels gain supernatural power; and, the very bewitchment of the Goddess of Wealth. (1.42)

Who can fathom religious hypocrisy's course, like that of a fish in the deep. It too has no hands or feet or head, and is most indiscernible. (1.43)

Serpents are captivated through the power of *mantras*; innocent antelope, by snares; birds, by nets; men, through religious hypocrisy. (1.44)

All hail religious hypocrisy! It is the mockery of human intellect; the very basis of deception; the cause of the world's ruin; Misperception [personified]; and, the very basis of fraudulent enterprises' success! (1.45)

In the complex and constantly grinding wheel of worldly existence (*saṃsāra*), deceitful religious hypocrisy is both the nave and the ground it travels over. (1.46)

The tree of religious hypocrisy has the closing of eyes as its root; it draws its moisture from Brāhmaṇas' sacred locks, dripping from their ritual bathing; it flowers into ritual purity, and its many branches have hundreds of [Brāhmaṇical] comforts as their fruits. (1.47)

In the ostentatious observance of a vow, there is the religious hypocrisy of a *heron*;[13] in keeping things concealed, there is the religious hypocrisy of a turtle; in keeping one's eyes expressionless, there is the sinister religious hypocrisy of a cat. (1.48)

The heron's religious hypocrisy is a masterly hypocrisy; the turtle's religious hypocrisy is a kingly hypocrisy; but, the cat's religious hypocrisy is the world conqueror of hypocrisies! (1.49)

Whosesoever nails, beard and hair are kept very short; whosesoever beard is long or locks are matted; whosoever gobbles clay like a Piśāca; whosoever keeps a vow of silence; whosesoever feet are barely covered. . . (1.50)

Whosesoever golden necklace is an enormously knotted sacred thread hung across his back; whosesoever arms are frozen—like those of a pot—by the folds of his garment crammed into his armpits. . . (1.51)

Whosesoever learnedness (*pāṇḍityam*) is promoted by quarrels of every king and finger-wagging forensics; whosesoever lips publicly tremble in prayer (*japa*); whosoever shows himself lost in religious meditation upon city crossroads. . . (1.52)

Whosoever touches his ear in ritual gesture; by whomsoever everyone at a sacred bathing place is kept waiting by his repeated and prolonged immersions and ritual sipping of water with his hand cupped in a stage-gesture. . . (1.53)

Whosesoever austere ritual bathing at winter's end is announced by his chattering teeth; whosesoever elaborate worship of the gods is proclaimed by his smearing a great *tilaka*-mark on his forehead. . . (1.54)

Whosoever wears a flower on his head[14] while shifting his glance from side to side like a crow [to be sure that all see it][15]—that sort of person is to be known as a religious hypocrite! (1.55)

The religious hypocrite is a glory-seeking scoundrel who is submissive before a worthless man; is arrogant before a virtuous one; and, by sentiment, is an enemy to his kinsmen and a kinsman to his enemy. (1.56)

When the time arrives to do his duty, the religious hypocrite bows his head and proffers instead a hundred blandishments; his duty done, he becomes pitiless, frowning and keeping silent. (1.57)

There are hypocritical pretences of ritual purity, of quietism, of being a graduate of a Brahmanical education, and also of yogic contemplation (*samādhi*); but, more than a hundred times worse is the hypocritical pretension of indifference to the world! (1.59)

Caviling at the conduct of the holy; expending huge amounts of clay in ritual purification; touching only one's own kinsmen—by these hypocritical pretensions of ritual purity a man becomes a second Viśvāmitra. (1.60)

The legendary Submarine Fire (*vaḍavāgni*) insatiably and indiscriminately digests materials of every kind; the hypocritical pretension of non-violence is also omnivorous: it craves valuables left in its safe-keeping and robs its victims of every sort of good sense. (1.61)

Whether shaven-headed or wearing an ascetic's matted locks; whether naked or shaded by a royal parasol; whether carrying a sceptre (*daṇḍa*)[16] or ochre-robed—his asceticism proclaimed by the ashes smeared on his body, the lecher of religious hypocrisy flourishes in every quarter! (1.62)

Whether bald and fat or with the withered frame of a monk; whether his head is wrapped in a rag or surrounded by the turrets of a *caitya* hall—Greed is the aged sire of religious hypocrisy; Artifice, its mother; Fraud, its brother; Deceptive Appearance, its wife; Menace, its son. (1.63-4)

Once upon a time, the Self-born Lord (Brahmā), having finished the creation of all the worlds and their creatures, remained pensive for some time, having nothing more to do. (1.65)

His divine vision told him that mortal men fell short of enjoying money and other comforts, due to their peculiar adherence to sincerity. (1.66)

With eyes closed and mind fixed in his yogic state of creative illusion (*māyā*), he created Religious Hypocrisy—the very foundation of worldly esteem—for the enrichment of mankind. (1.67)

[Religious Hypocrisy] wore a tuft of *kuśa* grass; carried a book, a rosary, an empty water-pot, a staff (*daṇḍa*), a black antelope skin, a shovel and a horn as crooked as his own heart. (1.68)

His ear and hand were more than thickly adorned with sacred *kuśa* grass. On his well-displayed shaven head he wore a white flower fixed at the base of his Brāhmaṇical lock and ringed with still more *kuśa*. (1.69)

His neck was rigid as a pole. His lips were flapping in prayer (*japa*). His eyes were screwed up to indicate yogic contemplation (*samādhi*). His hand was braceleted with rosary beads. And he carried a vessel full of clay. (1.70)

Keeping silent, he spoke his whole mind by every manner of contemptuous gesture, by angry glances and by menacing and frowning facial expressions. (1.71)

Keeping himself pure and guarding against the pollution of another's touch—even in Brahmā's heaven!—Religious Hypocrisy remained standing in front of his father, though he craved a seat. (1.72)

His stupendous paraphernalia swiftly intimidated the Seven Divine Sages: they stood before him with their hands held in a reverential gesture. (1.73)

Brahmā—for whom the whole sweep of the universe's creation was mere child's play—saw him and stood both shaken with excitement and petrified at the same time: wondering at his son's weightiness. (1.74)

The sage Agastya was thunderstruck at Religious Hypocrisy's exceedingly severe pious observances. The sage Vaśiṣṭha hunched his back in embarrassment at his own comparatively paltry vows and ascetic practices. (1.75)

The sage Kautsa too shrunk with shame, reproaching himself for his own elementary monastic vows. Nārada too, his own austerities lacking [Religious Hypocrisy's] ostentation, lost his self-respect. (1.76)

Jamadagni hid his face between his knees. Viśvāmitra trembled. Gālava hung his head. Even Bhṛgu was overcome with embarrassment. (1.77)

[Religious Hypocrisy] craved a seat, yet he stood bolt upright before [his father]. His fat, irritable body was unmoving; his eye, angrily riveted on a lotus seat. (1.78)

Knowing his son craved a seat, Brahmā—his smile illuminating his own *haṃsa* perch with the brightness of his teeth—lovingly spoke: (1.79)

'Sit down, Son, here on my lap. You merit [this privilege] by virtue of your exceptional and wonderful piety, consistent with the dignity arising from a host of worthy qualities. (1.80)

So addressed by the Creator of the Universe, Religious Hypocrisy—reluctantly, feeling some misgivings[17]—attempted to purify Brahmā's lap by sprinkling it with a handful of holy water and forced himself to sit down. (1.81)

Religious Hypocrisy declared: 'Certainly, if something needs saying, it need not be said so loudly; but only after covering Your mouth with Your hand, so that I might not be touched by bits of Your breath!' (1.82)

Observing [Religious Hypocrisy's] unequalled purity with a smile, Brahmā shook his finger vigorously and declared: 'You *are* Religious Hypocrisy!' (1.83)

'Get up! Descend to the sea-girt earth and enjoy there pleasures unknown to even the wise!' (1.84)

Formally dismissed in this way by Brahmā, Religious Hypocrisy tied a mill-stone about his neck and descended to the world of mortals who founder in the ocean of worldly existence (*saṃsāra*). (1.85)

Reaching the mortal world and wandering through its forests and cities, Religious Hypocrisy implanted his victory-banner in the land of the Gauḍas[18] and freely roamed to the points of the compass. (1.86)

Religious Hypocrisy flourishes today in the speech of the Bactrians, in the pious observance of vows among the Easterners and Southerners, in the government of the Kashmiris and everywhere among the Gauḍas!' (1.87)

Religious Hypocrisy's boon companions are those who at dawn paint a *tilaka* mark [on their foreheads] with ashes or powders obtained for performing obsequies merely for the sake of priestly remunerations. (1.88)

Religious Hypocrisy quickly split the earth's creatures into a thousand factions and now dwells visibly in the faces of judicial officers. (1.89)

Religious Hypocrisy himself first entered the hearts of *gurus*; then, the hearts of the immature; next, the hearts of those who practise religious austerities, the crooked hearts of officials, the hearts of religious initiates (*dīkṣita*), also the hearts of astrologers, physicians, servants, merchants, gold-smiths, dancers, soldiers, singers, orators and circuit beggars. (1.90-91)

Entering by degrees and in various guises the hearts of all creatures, Religious Hypocrisy finally entered into the birds and trees. (1.92)

Craving fish, the *heron*-ascetic performs austerities by standing on one foot in sacred waters—thus Religious Hypocrisy has even corrupted the birds! (1.93)

Craving water, the trees let their skins become weathered by the winds and wear the bark garments and matted hair of ascetics—this too is the spreading influence of Religious Hypocrisy! (1.94)

One should always be aware that Religious Hypocrisy is all-pervading and all-plundering. Only when it is understood in all its diversity will the ploys of the deceitful be in vain. (1.95)

Religious Hypocrisy is the very wishing-tree of the crowd of deceitful men. Long ago Viṣṇu was able to stride across the three worlds through the sanctimonious hypocrisy of a dwarf![19] (1.96)

On the strength of this passage alone, I think it fair to say that Kṣemendra had no special esteem for Brāhmaṇas.

Kṣemendra on Counterfeit Gurus and Their Devotees

Like quack physicians and corrupt bureaucrats, the *gurus* in Kṣemendra's satires lay waste mankind (*N.* 2.77). In Kṣemendra's view, an eminent *guru* is nothing better than an all-devouring, night-feeding, malignant spirit (*yakṣa*) who sustains himself with stolen wealth and wives (*N.* 2.103). Like worldly existence, his character is purely illusory and, again like the world whose faults he epitomizes, he is obsessed with lust and hatred, is dangerous on account of his greed and hypocrisy, and is motivated only by his own petty self-interest (*Deś.* 8.2). At best, he offers the promise of a cheaply-bought personal salvation (*Deś.* 8.3)—the comfort of which they purchase dearly; at worst, he caters to their much more venal interests. The *modus operandi* of such 'gurus of the cross roads' is to win followers through the display of a little *yoga* and to win subservience through awe-inspiring though worthless initiations (*dīkṣās*); they are in reality hunters whose object is to pick off the wives and possessions of the innocent. (*K.* 9.15)

The most useful tool of such *gurus* in blinding their devotees to their obvious faults is the skilful hypocritical pretension to spiritual eminence. Thinking their *guru* a saint, devotees are apt to rationalize pride, hypocrisy, greed, deception, cheating and lechery (*N.* 2.102). Yet, even if the physical appearance and personal habits of such men be considered objectively for a moment, the devotees should know better; such is certainly the case with the great Śaiva *guru* described in the *Narmamālā*. True enough, his forehead is always moist from the application of *tilaka* marks (2.104); true enough, what little hair remains on his bald head is matted and tied in a preposterously tiny braid (2.105); true enough, his ears are daubed with saffron—yet, for all this affected parade of holiness, he remains a glassy-eyed, lantern-jawed, pot-bellied, stuttering blowhard whose facial expressions—(if you can forgive Kṣemendra for saying so)—are those of an old she-buffalo's pudenda (2.105-9). His throat is a drainage-ditch capable of emptying a wine-jug instantly (2.107). The meditation-cloth with which he wraps his fat chest is soiled and reeking of meat and drink. His swollen belly, stuffed with sweets, cakes and fish, is set off grotesquely by a cavernous navel filled with red *sindūra*-powder (2.109). The man is indeed a *guru* in every sense but that which benefits others: he is obese (*guru*), thick (*guru*) of voice, sluggish (*guru*) in his slothfulness and stupidity, monstrous (*guru*) in his oversized buttocks, belly and gullet. He knows well how to extort money from officials enamoured of prostitutes: an art in which he is qualified to be a teacher (*guru*)—how is it that this Śaiva can be a *guru* in so many ways and still turn up light of good conduct and the lessons of Śiva (2.112)?

Incredibly enough, it is *this guru* who is invited to cure the wife of a prominent official. Of course, the wife's illness is as fraudulent—(her remarkable faithlessness during her husband's recent absence has so cooled her ardour towards him that she shams an illness in order to avoid his attentions)—as her husband is corrupt. None the less, the husband is willing to bear the expenses of inviting the *guru* and his henchmen to perform a sacrifice in order to restore his wife to normal health. There is nothing surprising in this: the *guru* has built up a considerable renown and the corrupt official is nothing if not a believer in religious expediency. He had been a Buddhist, but became a

Vaiṣṇava for the sake of ostentation. But now, for the sake of keeping his wife, he has developed a respect for the Kaula Tantra (2.101)!

A consummate showman, the *guru* makes his entrance to the ritual ground as dramatic as possible. Supported by a disciple at either arm, the *guru*, his eyes alternately closed or rolling in the affectation of spiritual ecstasy, comes in followed by a hundred disciples—like a fierce city-overlord come to plunder the place (3.11-12). A catalogue of his henchmen reveals what scoundrels with whom he chooses to ally himself. They are as follows: a leather-worker, a butcher, a potter, a fisherman, a market-place ascetic, an aged prostitute, a liquor dealer, an alcoholic bard, an elderly rake, five diseased libertines, a notorious cook, a beef-eating Śaivācārya, a mere weaver posing as a clan-*ācārya*, a noseless Śaivācārya, a naked *mauni*, another eccentric with bells on his knees which jingle when he sings hymns, a madman smeared with odure, a mountebank swathed in vines, an alchemist reciting *mantras* and still others who worship only the free food and drink of which they reek (3.13-18). And there can be little doubt that it is only for the sake of the latter that they attend the official's ceremony; before long, they have plundered everything edible, both cooked and raw (3.19). Eventually, they carry off large sacks containing the house's total provisions (3.20).

In contrast to the cynical rapacity of the *guru*'s henchmen is the superstitious behaviour of his devotees. Falling at his feet, they rock his throne by bumping the tops of their heads against its base (2.114). Kṣemendra warns against thinking such devotees to be ethical:

> *chandānuvartino ye śvabhrāpāte'pi sādhuvādaparāḥ |*
> *sarvasvahāriṇaste madhurā viṣavad viśantyantaḥ ||*
>
> 'Those "sweet" people who hang on the words of a "Saint" and conform to his will—even to the point of plunging into the Śvabhra Hell—like poison, they insinuate themselves and carry off all that is precious. (K. 9.42).

The venal concerns of the *guru*'s clientele are the theme of the eighth part of the *Deśopadeśa*. The *guru* they approach is equally as sinister as that of the *Narmamālā* considered above.

One of his initiates is a chief clerk who does not scruple to rob the gods, 'twice-born', cities and towns—even villages and goatherd-stations! He approaches the *guru* in the interest of gaining still more booty (8.5). Another of the *guru*'s initiates is the respectable wife, who spurns her husband only to play the *guru*'s whore (8.8-10). The third initiate is a drunken bard. The fourth is a crooked merchant seeking further prosperity. The *guru* was created to siphon off the money this villain has accumulated through cheating his customers (8.16). Fifth, a hack poet comes seeking eloquence. The sixth is a decrepit alchemist who seeks an elixer of youth. Ruined by quicksilver and beset by terminal dysentery, the old fool ecstatically thinks his body finally purified (8.22)! Seventh is a crooked gambler. Though he cheats at the game, he is still frequently penniless. He seeks from the *guru* a *mantra* to propitiate Gaṇeśa, the god of good luck (8.23-5). Eighth is a typical *buddhivihinaḥ śiṣyaḥ* or disciple lacking a mind of his own. He is a *kevalabhakta*, a devotee first and last. Lacking independent judgement, he only follows the trodden path, like a dumb beast (8.26). Ninth is a hypocritical devotee. He plants his head at his *guru*'s feet only for the sake of the food and drink he enjoys through his religious hypocrisy (8.27-29). A *vīṇā*-playing disciple is tenth. Believing that he plays divinely, he hungers for adulation. Instead, his poor playing offends his listeners' ears (8.30-2). Eleventh is a quack physician. He knows his craft but little; he is more of a plague to mankind than a benefactor. In this he is inferior to his *guru*—who at least is able to rid his disciples of their disease of money (8.33-5). Twelfth is a flea-bitten petty clerk. A host of kinsmen have prevailed upon him to use his office to support them. Consequently, a mass of bad debts will bring him to court within a year. He has reason to fear public punishment (8.36-8). Thirteenth is a *paṇḍita* who hilariously affects learning. His aim is to be treated with the respect of a *guru* among fools and, to this end, gives every one a headache with his sesquipedalian, nasalized locutions. Kṣemendra describes the extent of his education in a stanza full of puns:

> *vidvānasādhuśabdo vismṛtaliṅgo napuṃsakaprakṛtiḥ |*
> *aviditasakalasamāso satsu sadā dvandvameva jānāti*[20] || (8.41)

On the grammatical level, the verse means as follows: 'This

"learned man", whose grammar is faulty; whose grammar is forgotten; by whom an uninflected crude form of a word is mistaken for a neuter; who knows little of the whole grammar of compounds—he finds copulative compounds among this terminations of the present participle! A very clever verse in which double meanings are given to the following seven technical terms of Sanskrit grammar: *śabda*, *liṅga*, *napuṃsaka*, *prakṛti*, *samāsa*, *sat* and *dvandva*. The verse can also be read as follows: this coarse-spoken "learned man" has forgotten [his own] sex; is neuter by nature; is ignorant of all that relates to intercourse; and, knows only continual quarreling with good people.'[21] The fourteenth attendant of the *guru* is a wicked scribe whose omissions and additions of a few lines inspire terror among the learned (8.43-5). Fifteenth is a repulsive ascetic whose matted hair, we learn, serves as the footstool of prostitutes (8.47). Sixteenth and last is a widow, who links up with the *guru*—at her dead husband's funeral rites—with predictable results (cf. 8.50).

Perhaps the most appropriate way of concluding this section is to note that Kṣemendra prays for the success of those men of integrity who do not serve *gurus*, the repositories of corruption (*N*. 2.113).

Kṣemendra on Kāyastha Bureaucrats

Lest it be thought that Kṣemendra's satire was directed solely at members of the religious professions, we shall consider his treatment of Kāyastha bureaucrats last. Actually, we have already seen references to corrupt goldsmiths, astrologers, physicians, scribes and so forth; yet, so far there has not been enough emphasis on the last half of Kosambi's pairing of 'monastery and court'. The degree to which Kāyastha bureaucrats tyrannized Kashmir for centuries will be treated when we consider Kalhaṇa below. Suffice it to say that their power during the centuries before and after Kṣemendra was such that we may take it that his attacks on this group constituted something supposedly absent in Sanskrit literature: namely, biting satire directed against abuse of office.

Nor was Kṣemendra's invective against Kāyastha bureaucrats limited to a few offhand remarks: they receive a whole chapter in the *Kalāvilāsa* and, as if that were not enough, they are the principal target of the whole *Narmamālā*. In fact, it might be fair to say that in terms of sheer numbers of satiric verses (—let alone the intensity of their rancour—) the Kāyasthas constituted Kṣemendra's favourite target.

The great majority of Kṣemendra's attacks upon Kāyasthas are directed against the rapacious corruption which invariably marks their administration. Thus, he begins the fifth chapter of his *Kalāvilāsa* with the observation that deception personified dwells in the mouth and written records of the Kāyasthas. (1) As the demon Rāhu devours the full orb of the moon, so Kāyasthas seize every bit of a bountiful crop of grain in total. (2) Although a realized *yogī* may have plumbed all the wiles of earthly existence, nevertheless no one can fathom the wiles of a Kāyastha chief-clerk. (3) In their rapacity, they are comparable to night-roaming *piśāca* demons. (5) The weeping of the Prosperity of a Kingdom (here personified as a goddess) with tears stained black from the collyrium about her eyes is said to flow as ink from their penpoints as they rob her. (7) The chief-clerk, again, is compared to Citragupta:[22] by the mere erasure of a line, he can make a prosperous man a pauper. (11) They bring about such deprivation of livelihood through their own special, perfected *mantra*: the word 'No!' (18)

After these observations describing the faults of Kāyasthas, Kṣemendra tells a didactic tale imparting his view of their irredeemably flawed character. The story opens with the introduction of a ne'er-do-well whose thievery of money, domestic animals and even apparel has caused everyone, including his own kinsmen to disown him. He takes flight to a Śaiva Shrine, no doubt hoping to avoid prosecution for his crimes. There he begins the worship of Śiva in a offhand way, having nothing else to occupy his time. As time passes, he becomes engrossed in his worship: spending sleepless nights in meditation, chanting hymns, praying and lighting lamps before the image. After he had thus performed a multitude of meritorious acts, Śiva felt disposed to speak to his devotee through the temple image which, being a *tāntrika* icon, was garlanded with human skulls. Just as the god was beginning to confer a boon upon the reformed scoundrel, one of the many skulls comprising his necklace created such a commotion that the god was forced to break off in mid-sentence. When Śiva fell silent, his devotee discreetly retired to take a ritual bath. In his absence, Śiva hurriedly interrogated the noisome skull, asking its motive in creating such a disturbance. The skull points out that the devotee's worship and offerings of food, incense and flowers all stem from his wretched state of failure in human society. Only a miserable man, the skull declares, becomes an ascetic; only a destitute man becomes respectful; only one whose wealth and authority have collapsed becomes humble before all and soft-spoken. It is only the less fortunate of men who conduct themselves as they should; what shall we say of the dutifulness of those intoxicated with the wine of their own wealth? Those who have attained their goals lose their utility as servants. If this scoundrel is satisfied, who will bring offerings to this deserted place? The skull thus concludes his speech with a plea to Śiva to condemn his devotee to a life of perpetual servitude, forever banished from his home and kinsmen.

Hearing this crooked reasoning, Śiva demands the skull to identify himself. The skull replies that he had formally lived in a Kāyastha family, but chose to neglect his bureaucratic duties in favour of a life of ritual bathing, prayer, vows, pilgrimage, and sacred study. From the copious merit thus accumulated, the skull was honoured with a place in Śiva's garland after death. When he heard all this, Śiva declared 'Truly, you *are* a Kāyastha! Though reduced to a skull, you still cannot leave duplicity!' So saying, Śiva rewarded his devotee and banished that meddlesome skull from the uppermost row of his garland.[23]

Greater acerbity characterizes the satire of Kāyasthas in the *Narmamālā*. The whole of this work is devoted to the humorous narration of the career and downfall of a corrupt Kāyastha.[24] The work purportedly recreates the politically and ethically bankrupt state of Kashmir previous to the ascension to the throne of Ananta (A.D. 1028-63), whose reign coincided closely with Kṣemendra's literary career (A.D. 1015-66). It is ironic that Kṣemendra's declaration that Ananta reduced the corruption of these rapacious bureaucrats to the status of a mere memory[25] proved to be more sanguine than lastingly true: the *Rājataraṅgiṇī* informs us that the Kāyasthas were able to find favour with one of Ananta's best-loved Sahi princes and in characteristic fashion under this king also.[26] History does not inform us of whether or not the Kāyasthas were able to revenge themselves upon Kṣemendra for the caustic satire he directed at them in the *Narmamālā* and other writings. Doubtless, they must have cherished a keen desire to do so.

In his *Narmamālā*, Kṣemendra traces the lineage of the Kāyasthas to the chief accountant of the demonic *daityas*. After the defeat of the *daityas* at the hands of Viṣṇu, Kali (the personification of discord in the present age) took pity on the chief accountant and armed him with a new and powerful weapon, the pen, with which he might oppress gods and virtuous men.

The central characters or 'heroes' of this 'Kāyasthacarita' are characterized as thorough religious hypocrites. One is pictured attending a Śaiva shrine in the company of his henchmen. There, as tears flow down his cheeks in the chanting of verses from the *Stavacintāmaṇi*, he inquires *sotto voce* of the progress made to date in his oppression of the Brāhmaṇas who oppose him at the shrine of Vijayeśvara:

> How many were made to fast until death yesterday? . . . Let those who died in fasting be dragged away by ankle-chains. Loose the house-burning officials into the villages! After all is plundered, let those opposing the fines be slain!

He concludes his two-faced monologue with the observation that citizens are like *guggula* seeds, which exude a perfume when crushed.[27]

The next Kāyastha to be described is a *paripālaka* or Provincial Governor. He is an immense man whose arrogant contempt for others matches his protruding belly. His dreadful temper is compared to a calamitous disease. He is the scourge of temples and villages alike, appropriating to himself temple-offerings, killing priests and cattle, murdering the heads of households and stripping the village women bare.[28]

The Provincial Governor's chief-clerk is of a similar cast. Nearly as arrogant as his master, he uses his office to amass a personal fortune. Now both he and his wife flaunt their ill-gotten affluence before the very citizens from whom it was coerced. In this respect, the chief-clerk is like the Superintendent of Finances, whose considerable wealth stems from the illegal appropriation of land-grants made to Brāhmaṇas. It is also his practice to empty temple-granaries, selling the booty in the open market. He then realizes a double profit by forcing the temples to restock their stores with grain which he sells at an outrageous price. He boasts of having melted down a large temple-bell, replacing it with a tiny one and turning the rest into copper pots which he sold for his own profit. He advises his master that theft is possible at every step in the overseeing of temple finances. He boasts further of having reduced the honest officials who opposed him to a condition of starvation. In his administration of finances, he is compared by Kṣemendra to an old rat who picks a walnut clean.[29]

Next comes an official with the simple title of Niyogī. Though his title does not tell us much, Kṣemendra makes it clear that he is a powerful executive officer with broad magisterial powers in the supervision of civil and criminal cases. Dressed in white, he rides through the villages causing the villagers to jump from his way. Kṣemendra compares him to an old white crane bent on swallowing up the village fish. Like the rest of his colleagues, he has made himself rich at the citizens' expense. He uses his magisterial powers to confiscate property on a large scale. The populace has been reduced to submission through his arbitrary administration of justice and capricious sentences of imprisonment and corporal punishment. He is pictured tearing to shreds letters commuting the punishment of a wretch who stands before him pleading for mercy. With his characteristic attention to official hypocrisy, Kṣemendra depicts the Niyogī as a gourmand who contents himself two small dollops of saltless mung lentils when a representative of the king is present. On the village level, the Niyogī employs a skilled forger to be of aid in contract disputes.[30]

It is the Niyogī whose unfaithful wife's pretense of illness leads eventually to the employment of the fraudulent *guru* described in the previous section of this chapter. Her father is described as an officer of the court so unscrupulous that he contemplates the confiscation of his son-in-law's house when he attends the *guru*'s bogus ritual designed to rid his daughter of her ailment. Kṣemendra depicts him as a hypocrite whose affectation of humility masks a greedy and corrupt heart. Moreover, he is depicted as a Brāhmaṇa whose morning rituals reflect nocturnal drinking and whoring more than a desire to maintain ritual purity. As a hypocritical Brāhmaṇa, he more fears to begin his day with the sight of a learned Brāhmaṇa than to see an outcaste upon a manure-strewn path. He leaves for court each morning surrounded by pitiful bankrupts come to plead for mercy, contentedly looking forward to the day's bribes. Kṣemendra calls him a monster thriving in a sea of legalities.[31]

On his visit to his son-in-law's house, the Officer of the Court is attended by his Chief Clerks. Kṣemendra hails them as gods of cosmic retribution who help themselves to the world's moveable and immoveable property. They are like swarming fish, to whom the properties of bankrupt wretches are like offerings cast upon the waters of judicial proceedings. At their deceitful word, a failed man is made successful and a successful man a failure. But throughout it all, the Chief Clerks pursue only their own greedy aims: they would even steal a man's heart. Without bribes, they become seeing blind men, speaking mutes and the hearing deaf. They make a thorough study of human weakness and use their knowledge to protect the corrupt while bankrupting the good.[32]

Shortly after the *guru*'s disastrous ritual, the Niyogī falls from power. Voltaire declared that there is nothing so ignominious as to be obscurely hanged, but the degradation of the Niyogī's end is worse. When surrounded by arresting soldiers, he urinates helplessly out of fear. His entire property is confiscated. After rotting long in rigorous imprisonment, he is eventually freed through the manipulations of his prostitute sister. Though now thoroughly repentant, he is a pauper. Abandoned by his worthless wife, he wanders through the homes of his kinsmen, seeking a crumb. Turned out to wander aimlessly, racked by disease, his legs and knees eaten away by dogs, he stumbles and falls into a pit of excrement. Even a woman who offers water to passers-by turns him away, mistaking him for a low-caste Ḍomba.[33] Outcastes burn his eyebrows and beard off by thrusting his face into a firepot. Fallen into yet another pit of human excrement, he gives up his life in a degraded manner which mocks the arrogance of his corrupt life.[34]

Though our taste may well question the amusement afforded by the conclusion of Kṣemendra's *mālā* of *narmas*, we must admit that the satire of corrupt officials in it rivals in intensity anything produced in ancient, medieval or renaissance Europe. Yet, Kṣemendra was not the first Kashmiri—to voice criticism of official corruption. In the early ninth century, Dāmodaragupta compared the constituent elements of state government with prostitutes in the seizure of vast amounts of money.[35] He also draws attention to the expenditure of public funds on prostitutes.[36] But what is more interesting in Kṣemendra's satire of corrupt Kāyasthas is M.A. Stein's contention that 'the great mass of them [—the Kashmiri—Kāyasthas—] was *undoubtedly* Brahman by caste, corresponding to the present Kārkun of Kashmir.'[37] We have already seen above how the Niyogī's father-in-law, the Officer of the Court, was depicted as hypocritically devoted to the Brāhmaṇical morning ritual complete with clay and sacred *darbha* grass. Moreover, the Kāyastha's skull's account of putting aside bureaucratic duties for pious solemnities on the bank of the Gaṅgā (as related in the *Kalāvilāsa*) could conceivably be seen as the return to the more common caste occupation of a Brāhmaṇa. Be this as it may, Stein's remark, if accurate, makes even more doubtful Dattaray's assertion of Kṣemendra's high esteem for Brāhmaṇas. Furthermore, it is obvious that there is good reason for suspecting that many if not all of Kṣemendra's counterfeit *gurus* were of the same caste. My own conclusion is that Kṣemendra, like the author of the *Pañcatantra*, may well have respected certain Brāhmaṇas, but fell far short of absolute reverence for the caste taken as a whole.

There is also little doubt that Kṣemendra meant his satires to expose real faults within his society. Speaking of disparagement of Kāpālika ascetics in Sanskrit literature, Hara Minoru has recently written as follows: 'Despite the presence of these references to Kāpālikas and some detailed descriptions of Kāpālika doctrines and practices in Sanskrit literature, one should be careful not to put too much trust in this literary evidence, because the figures presented in Sanskrit Kāvya, dramas and Kathā literature are often artificial and stereotyped under the restrictions of the poetic conventions (a sort of *kavi-samaya*) and the rules of dramaturgy.'[38] In return, I think the literary *and* historical context of Kṣemendra's attacks require that we should not put too much trust in caveats of this sort. If we turn to the ninth *sarga* of the *Kalāvilāsa* ('Characterization of Various Scoundrels'), we find vigorous criticism of many varieties of social parasites presented in a context quite free from the requirements of sustaining a narrative. The context makes it clear that Kṣemendra really does mean to warn his society against the machinations of quack physicians, alchemists, astrologers, counterfeit *gurus*, cheating gamblers, corrupt judges, demagogues, sychophants, disciples who do their *guru*'s iniquitous work—even pandering Buddhist nuns. In his satires, Kṣemendra's aim was always to impart sincere instruction (*upadeśa*) to his country (*deśa*).[39]

Kalhaṇa: The Historian as Social Critic

Like Kṣemendra, Kalhaṇa is openly critical of Kāyasthas in his *Rājataraṅgiṇī*.[40] It is fortunate that his work survived (unlike Kṣemendra's *Nṛpāvali*), for it provides the historical background for much of Kṣemendra's social criticism and shows that many of the problems Kṣemendra renders there plagued Kashmir long before his birth and for some time after his death. Kalhaṇa's treatment of the Kāyasthas is a case in point. He blames them for the corruption of King Jayāpīḍa. Under their influence Jayāpīḍa turns from the honourable means of acquiring wealth (such as foreign conquest) and heeds their advice to plunder his own countrymen. He begins to levy exorbitant taxes and becomes increasingly greedy through the instigation of his officers of finance. From that time onward, Kalhaṇa tells us, the kings of Kashmir looked to Kāyasthas for guidance.[41] The king's mind was so turned by greed that he regarded the Kāyasthas—who plundered all and returned almost nothing—to be his true benefactors. Brāhmaṇas who objected were slain by the hundreds.[42]

Needless to say, subsequent kings were also corrupted by their Kāyastha officials. Kalhaṇa tells us that Śaṅkaravarman (A.D. 883-902) let them loose to plunder the wealth of the virtuous, and was sullied by this misdeed. He informs us further that this king's own son complained to his father that his Kāyastha-inspired oppression of the populace has left them with the activity of breathing as their sole remaining vital function.[43] Similarly, the psychopathic King Unmattāvanti (A.D. 937-39) let loose the Kāyasthas upon his land already plundered by the Ḍāmaras.[44] That Kṣemendra's favourite, King Ananta, also yielded to this temptation has been already mentioned above. Kalhaṇa continues, telling us that King Harṣa (A.D. 1089-1101) utilized the Kāyasthas to impose such great fines that not even a clod of earth was left behind.[45]

This tradition of official corruption was broken under Uccala

(A.D. 1101-11). Kalhaṇa tells of a purge of the Kāyasthas under that king with evident approval. He says that Uccala bore in mind a verse from the *Manusmṛti* to the effect that appointed officials are murderous creatures, thieves villains, and even demons.[46] Kalhaṇa goes on to compare such officials with plagues, crabs (which supposedly kill their own fathers), white ants (which supposedly kill their mothers), poisonous trees and vampiric *vetālas*. He lists in some detail the public humiliations visited upon the deposed Kāyasthas, but notes that they were so unregenerate as to prostitute their own mothers, sisters, daughters and wives in the hope of winning employment from the *samantas*. The wise, says Kalhaṇa, thought much of the mighty king's swift retribution directed towards the corrupt Kāyasthas.[47]

The rule of justice under Uccala was of such merit that Kalhaṇa, in describing it, is brought to employ the image of another Kṛta Age. Yet, scarcely a year after Uccala's death, the Kāyasthas were reinstated by King Sussala (A.D. 1112-20). A treacherous Kāyastha named Gauraka was made Prime Minister. On account of his gentle demeanour, his viciousness went unperceived by the public. Once again the people were over-taxed so that official corruption might flourish.[48]

Like Kṣemendra again, Kalhaṇa appears to have had little respect for the *gurus* of Kashmir. This is evident in his description of another period of relative justice under Yaśaskara (A.D. 939-48). Under his supervision, Brāhmaṇas kept to their studies and forswore bearing arms. Their *gurus* ceased to drink liquor when they chanted the *Sāmaveda*, nor did they seek to upset sacred philosophical traditions with vain works of their own composition. Nor did errant wives continue to spurn their husbands after participating in the *gurus*' sham *dīkṣās*.[49]

The corruption of Ananta's son and heir Kalaśa is described candidly. Kalhaṇa associates the crown-prince's moral demise with a number of parasites, including three *gurus* who schooled him in depravity. One of these, the Brāhmaṇa *guru*, Pramadakaṇṭha, is characterized as a panderer who lived in open incest with his daughter. The second was a faith-healer known as the 'Cat-Merchant.' The third was another Brāhmaṇa called Loṣṭaka, a charlatan who apparently acted as a *guru*, procurer and soothsayer for the young king.[50] When Kalaśa dies a coward's death,

Kalhaṇa remarks that his end renders ridiculous the arrogance engendered by the spiritual instructions of his *gurus*.[51]

Although Kalhaṇa was almost certainly a Brāhmaṇa, he does not stint to relate with disapproval accounts of their political machinations.[52] In summing up his general attitude in this regard, M.A. Stein notes that 'various references show that whatever respect traditional notions demanded for the 'gods of the earth' *in abstracto*, Kalhaṇa was not prepared to extend it to their claims as a political factor.'[53]

The Kathāsaritsāgara

Two Kashmiri, Kṣemendra and Somadeva (twelfth century) recast Guṇāḍhya's *Bṛhatkathā* into Sanskrit. Although I argued above that Hara Minoru's caveat against taking stock literary character too seriously does not apply to Kṣemendra's satires, the warning doubtless finds greater applicability in the consideration of both Kṣemendra's and Somadeva's adaptations of Guṇāḍhya's great collection of tales. In these there *are* narratives—many of a stock variety—to be sustained. Therefore, the tales of these collections must have limited value as documents of social criticism, let alone as purposeful attacks against the perceived faults within the author's *own* societies. Here the authors' *primary* intention must have been to simply tell stories, not to impart lessons.

In the *Kathāsaritsāgara*,[54] we are given the now familiar motif of a scoundrel affecting asceticism for the purpose of swindling ordinary folk. This is what happens in the tale of a thief named Śiva who shows himself absorbed in pious observances by day, but ponders his victims' weaknesses by night. Śiva and his confederate, Mādhava, set out to rob a greedy, hypocritical Brāhmaṇa of his wealth and daughter. While Śiva continues his charade of asceticism, Mādhava pretends to be a Rajput possessed by a huge chest full of jewels. By starving himself for a few days, Mādhava shams fatal illness and calls upon the greedy Brāhmaṇa to find another of his caste whose piety is such that Mādhava may gain merit through the bequest of his great treasure. Naturally, Mādhava rejects all candidates until the Brāhmaṇa suggests that remarkable ascetic, Śiva. When the Brāhmaṇa approaches him, Śiva complains that he is a simple saint living a contented life and has no use for wealth. The greedy Brāhmaṇa, hoping to appropriate the fortune himself, admonishes Śiva that he should dutifully enter the second stage of life and swiftly engineers a marriage with his coveted daughter. Mādhava bestows his treasure chest—of fake jewels—upon Śiva who presses his new father-in-law to purchase it, claiming to have no use for precious stones. Thinking himself about to realize a windfall, the Brāhmaṇa swiftly trades his entire miser's fortune for the jewels and compels the exchange of signatures to insure the legality of the transaction.

Of course, in a story like this there is no social criticism implied of the sham ascetic. Indeed, Śiva and his accomplice are treated as heroes. The miserly Brāhmaṇa, it is true, is lampooned, but the story contents itself with a few ironies and the spectacle of his receiving a justly deserved swindling. The story of the Brāhmaṇa, Agniśarman, while plainly describing him to be such a fool that he welcomes bad omens as good, nevertheless treats him as a guileless blockhead who stumbles forward to a happy ending of his troubles. Female ascetics occasionally appear as procuresses,[55] but one is also seen in the role of an innocuous go-between.[56] Almost as innocuous is the Brāhmaṇa, Hariśarman, who shams powers of divination, but, when put to the test, wins great wealth through a most improbably serendipitous pair of accidents.[57] In another tale with similar elements, a Brāhmaṇa whose sole distinction is that he eats rice-husks is rewarded with a large sum of gold coins in recognition of his supposed austerity. Yet, the story continues by portraying him to be a pitiful miser who determines to kill himself when he loses his windfall.[58] Another tale in which a Brāhmaṇa is presented in a less than favourable light concerns two ascetics, one a Brāhmaṇa, the other an outcaste Cāṇḍāla. Both starve to death, but the outcaste exhibits more self-control, and is rewarded with a fortunate rebirth. The Brāhmaṇa craves forbidden food before his end, and is reborn to a degraded station.[59] Yet, at all times, these Brāhmaṇas are presented as flawed individuals, never as a class or even sub-class which the author seeks to discredit as a whole. And there are many stories in the *Kathāsaritsāgara* in which a Brāhmaṇa is portrayed as virtuous and noble.

One such story is worth mentioning because it tells, in passing, of kingly injustice. The hero of the tale is portrayed throughout as a model father, suffering long for his children's benefit.[60] The start of his many troubles comes when the kingdom in which he dwells suffers a severe drought. The response of the king, one Kamalavarman, is described as follows:

> *taddoṣeṇa ca rājātra prārebhe taskarāyitum |*
> *adharmeṇa prajābhyo'rthamākarṣanmuktasatpathaḥ ||*

Which states that on account of the drought the king began to play the thief, abandoned the path of right, and unjustly taxed his subjects.[61] As plainly critical as this verse is, we should probably not give much weight to this one *śloka* among the 24,000 which make up the collection. A capriciously brutal judge is the villain in another tale of a faultless brāhmaṇa and his chaste wife.[62]

As the *Kathāsaritsāgara* tales abound with magic of both a beneficient and malicious sort, it is not surprising to find there a number of stories featuring wicked ascetics intent on murdering innocent men in order to win occult powers. One such story has an ascetic present a box containing a jewel everyday to King Vikramāditya. With such an inducement, the king readily assents to the ascetic's request to meet him in a lonely spot to assist in the performance of an arcane ritual. But the god Viṣṇu intervenes and warns the king that the ascetic means to murder him. Nevertheless, the king keeps his appointment—only when the ascetic bids him to shut his eyes and sprawl at full length upon the ground ('by doing this, both of us will attain our ends'), the king pleads ignorance and asks the ascetic to demonstrate. When the ascetic only too gladly complies with the request, Vikramāditya cuts off his head.[63] In another tale, an ascetic actually succeeds in carrying off his ritual murder (an infanticide) and succeeds in winning kingship of the semi-divine *vidyādharas*. Yet, his glory proves to be short-lived, as the hero pursues him and causes the villain to fall to earth as helpless as before.[64]

We have already seen in the *Daśakumāracarita* a story in which a hapless ascetic (Marīci) succumbs to lust. In that instance, the fellow was more to be pitied than blamed. Quite different is a *Kathāsaritsāgara* tale in which a *guru* plots to kidnap and ravish the heroine. The lecher persuades the girl's father that she is endowed with inauspicious marks. The only way the father can prevent his own swift and certain death, says the *guru*, is to set the girl adrift on the Gaṅgā in a closed box. When the father reluctantly consents, the *guru* instructs his disciples to fetch the box and depart. All seemingly goes according to plan, but when the eager *guru* opens the box, a ferocious monkey leaps out and rids him of his nose and ears.[65]

This chapter on the considerable contribution of Kashmir to social criticism in Sanskrit literature might now be brought to a close. But, before doing so, it should be fitting to make mention of one final text which borrows extensively from the *Kathāsaritsāgara*.

The Bharaṭakadvātriṃśikā

The *Bharaṭakadvātriṃśikā* is a Jaina work which employs a number of tales from Somadeva's *Kathāsaritsāgara* with the aim of expounding the crooked ways of depraved Śaiva ascetics called Bharaṭakas.[66] The stories of this collection demonstrate, moreover, that Bharaṭakas are lecherous frauds, swindlers, liars and thieves. Although the author's name is unknown, we may be content that he had little love for Śaiva ascetics. As the product of an author with a poison pen, the work has been judged successful. Johannes Hertel has written that the collection of tales 'turns out to be a very clever and witty device, more effective at all events than a lot of big volumes of learned polemics would have been.'[67] Although, as Hertel maintains, the author knew his Sanskrit well, he has composed his work in an extremely simple Sanskrit style with frequent employment of Modern Indo-Aryan words. This fact, in my view, is of considerable significance, for it reveals the author's intention of using Sanskrit to reach a broad, popular audience. It should not, then, be possible to relegate this work to that class of Sanskrit texts designed to amuse the savants of 'the monastery and the court'.

Since the reader may feel that he has seen enough of lecherous *gurus* for one chapter, the stories below will concern the foolishness of the Bharaṭakas and their blockheaded disciples. Since a rather large proportion of the stories in this collection have this as their theme, this selection may be taken as fairly representative of the whole.

The first such story concerns a Bharaṭaka with the revealing name of Durmati (dim-wit). He is described as a parasite who gets his food supplied him by the whole populace of his town. One day he succeeds in gaining a lump of cold, curdled buffalo-milk from a householder, which gives him dreams that night. He dreams that his whole monastery is filled to the brim with delicious cooked food and things to drink. As he is the sole occupant of the place, he wonders what to do with the excess. With a mind not to let all this food spoil, he resolves to regain the good graces of the townspeople by inviting them to share his feast. As it happens, this day all the household hearths in the middle of the city have been doused,[68] so when Durmati comes there at noon, he finds a ravenously hungry mob. But when Durmati happily leads them to his place and throws open the door, he is shocked by the emptiness he perceives. He surveys every corner with agitated eyes, but to no avail. So, as if it were night again, he runs to his bed and crawls under his blanket, hoping to sleep—perchance to dream—again. When the grumbling mob demands to know why he fails to serve them, he says 'Wait a minute!' and explains the circumstances of his professed windfall. With this, the mob rises up angrily, denounces Durmati's dim-wittedness, and returns home, schooled in the lack of credibility of Bharaṭakas.[69]

Sometimes it is the Bharaṭaka *gurus* who suffer from the even greater stupidity of their disciples, as happens in this second tale. One such disciple, named Dhījaḍa (inert-cleverness), goes one day to the centre of town to beg some food. There he sees a carpenter straightening bamboo by soaking it in oil and bending it over a fire. It occurs to him that the same process might with benefit be applied to the crippled body of his ailing *guru*. As he proceeds accordingly a crowd gathers, summoned by the hapless *guru*'s moans. When they complain that Dhījaḍa is killing the poor fellow, he retorts that they are the foolish sons of foolish fathers. With this, the crowd raises an outcry and with considerable effort arrests Dhījaḍa's nonsensical therapy.[70]

Very similar is our third tale, in which a disciple goes to a physician to get medicine for his dying *guru*. The physician recommends something to serve as an antidote (*ativiṣam*) to the poisonous disease afflicting the *guru*. On the way back, the disciple's thoughts reveal him to have misunderstood the physician's recommendation: thinking that *ativiṣam* denotes a *powerful* poison, the disciple reasons that as his *guru* is now in a much weakened state, an ordinary poison would do. So the disciple promptly procures such a poison from the market, slays his *guru*, and wins the abuse of the citizenry.[71]

Our fourth tale involves an equally foolish disciple, but one whose mistake is less than fatal. His *guru* sends him to market to procure *ghee* (clarified butter) and oil. This he does, storing the *ghee* in one compartment of a two-sided incense censer with perforated lids. He puts the oil in the other side. When he returns home and is asked by his *guru* to show his purchases, the foolish disciple demonstrates, tipping the censer this way and that, successively spilling the contents of the each side onto the ground.[72]

Our fifth and last tale concerns an argument between two disciples over a lightning flash. The first correctly identifies the phenomenon, while the second maintains it to be a heavenly cart with fiery wheels. When the two cannot resolve their disagreement, they approach their *guru* to receive his judgement. The *guru* is abed, but, in order not to tarnish his affected omniscience, offers his own explanation. The sun, he explains, having covered its face (with clouds), is peering at the world. That being the case, the guru declares, it must be dawn and time to get up. The verse prefixed to the story commends students not to attribute profundity to their ignorant *gurus*.[73]

It must be clear from the above selections that the satire of the *Bharaṭakadvātriṃśikā* is of a rather broad and simple sort. Yet, it is these very qualities—together with the author's simplicity of diction—which suggest that the collection's criticism of Bharaṭaka ascetics probably found a widespread and appreciative audience.

References

1. Rajatbaran Dattaray, *A Critical Survey of Life and Works of Kṣemendra* (Calcutta: Sanskrit Pustak Bhandar, 1974).
2. Ibid., p. 68.
3. One most energetic self-promoter was the Kashmiri Śaiva saint, Abhinavagupta, who packs his colophons with puns on his own name.
4. Dattaray, loc. cit.
5. Such hyperbole is, of course, commonplace in *kāvya* literature. Cf. the

North Indian inscriptions in which the most modest titles begin with 'Mahārājādhirāja' and become rapidly much more prolix.

6. *JA*, S. VIII, T. VI, p. 401.

7. Dr. Suryakanta, *Kṣemendra Studies* (Poona; *OBA*, 1954), p. 9.

8. M.A. Stein, *Kalhaṇa's Rājataraṅgiṇī: A Chronicle of the Kings of Kashmir* (reprinted, Delhi: Motilal Banarsidass, 1961), vol. I, Introduction, p. 19.

9. Ibid., pp. 19-20.

10. A full-length study of Kṣemendra's satires is under way and translations are nearly finished.

11. For the role of Mūladeva in Sanskrit literature, cf. Maurice Bloomfield, 'The Character and Adventures of Mūladeva', *PAPS*, LII (1913), pp. 616-50.

12. That the term *dambha* denotes specifically *religious* hypocrisy may be gleaned from *Vācaspatyam*'s etymology of its derivative, *dhāmbhika* or 'hypocrite': '*dambhena carati dharmaṃ ṭhak*' stating that this kind of hypocrite is one who practises religion hypocritically. The allusion implicit in the etymology is to Pāṇini's *sūtra*, '*carati*' (4.4.8) calling for the *taddhita* suffix *ṭhak*, denoting that which is instrumental to the activity of the derived agent noun: here, one who cloaks his actions with *religious* hypocrisy.

13. Like certain ascetics, the *heron* stands motionless on one leg: all the better, according to Indian folklore, to deceive innocent fish. Cf *Vaka-Jātaka*.

14. By doing this he proclaims the fact that he has done his worship (*pūjā*).

15. In Sanskrit literature, the crow is supposed to have only a single eyeball which it rolls from socket to socket and thus it can never look straight ahead, but only to alternate sides. Cf V.S. Apte's *Practical Sanskrit Dictionary*, vol. III, Appendix E (*nyāyasaṅgraha*), p. 58, under *kākākṣigolakanyāya*.

16. The royal parasol and the *daṇḍa* staff are equally the attributes of kings and eminent *gurus*. *Bhogī* also means 'king'. The apparent confusion of kingly and ascetic attributes is deliberate: this device is known in Sanskrit rhetoric as *virodhābhāsa*. That the dominant sense is of an ascetic is proved by the ash-smeared body.

17. He so fears the ritual pollution of another's touch that he can barely force himself to sit in the lap of God!

18. Chiefly Bengal.

19. Due to the length of this passage, I thought it better not to include the Sanskrit text. The text I worked from may be found on pp. 222-28 of *Kṣemendralaghukāvyasaṁgraha*, ed. E. V.V. Raghavacharya and D.G. Padhye, number 7 in the Sanskrit Academy Series under the general editorship of Dr. Aryendra Sharma and published by the Sanskrit Academy, Osmania University, Hyderabad in 1961. It was also published in the *Kāvya-Mālā*, I, 1886, ed. Durgaprasad and K.P. Parab.

20. Here, for the first time, I depart from the text as printed in the *Kṣemendralaghukāvyasaṅgraha*, where two obvious mistakes occur in the first line: *sadbo* is written for *śabdo* and the end of this word is wrongly run together with the beginning of the next compound. A more correct version is found in the edition edited by Madhusudan Kaul Shastri, *KSTS*, no. 40 (Poona: 1923) *Deśopadeśa*, p. 30. This version, moreover, omits the *avagraha* which

the Hyderabad edition wrongly places before *satsu*. In his preface (p. 2), Kaul remarks that the copyist of the manuscript used 'seems to be a very careful writer.'

21. Cf. the following *kūṭa* or 'deceptive verse':

dvandvo dvigurapi cāham madgehe nityamavyayībhāvaḥ /
tatpuruṣa karma dhāraya yenāhaṃ syāṃ bahuvrīhiḥ //

This manages to incorporate the technical names of the six varieties of Sanskrit compounds. It may be translated as follows: 'Though I have two cows, I am married and in my house no money is ever spent. O man! Undertake that labour by which I may have much rice!' For the text and a brief Sanskrit commentary, cf. *SRB*, p. 189, number 51. It seems to me that Kṣemendra's attempt is both funnier and cleverer inasmuch as his wordplay works on two levels.

22. The legendary recorder employed by Yama, god of death.

23. The text of this story may be found in the *Kalāvilāsa*, 5.19–44 of either the Hyderabad or Poona editions.

24. Cf. *N.* 1.6: '*hāsāyātītakāyasthacaritam*.'

25. *N.* 1.4.

26. *RT* 7.149.

27. *N.* 1.39–44.

28. *N.* 1.62-70.

29. *N.* 1.72-96.

30. *N.* 1.97–127.

31. *N.* 2.117–32.

32. *N.* 2.133-41.

33. For Ḍombas, cf. the *Kathāsaritsāgara*, 12.96 ff.

34. *N.* 3.94–111.

35. *Kuṭṭanī-mata* 318.

36. Cf., Ajay Mitra Shastri, *India as Seen in the Kuṭṭanīmata of Dāmodaragupta* (Delhi: Motilal Banarsidass, 1975), pp. 53-54.

37. Italics added. Stein, op. cit., vol. I, Introduction, p. 19. Cf. also P.N.K. Bamzai, *A History of Kashmir* (New Delhi: Metropolitan Book Co. Ltd., 2nd revised edn. 1973), pp. 209-10.

38. Hara Minoru, Review of *The Kāpālikas and Kālāmukhas: Two Lost Saivite Sects* by David N. Lorenzen, *IIJ*, VII, Nos. 3/4 (Nov./Dec. 1975), p. 259.

39. Cf., the *Kalāvilāsa*, 10.42.

40. The references which follow are to the Sanskrit text of Kalhaṇa's *Rājataraṅgiṇī*, ed. Viśva Bandhu, et al. (Hoshiarpur: Vishveshvaranand Vedic Research Institute, 1963, 65 (2 vols.).

41. 4.621-3.

42. 4.629.

43. 5.180-84.

44. 5.439.

45. 7.1227.

46. Cf. the *Manusmṛti*, 7.123.

47. 8.85–122.

48. 8.560-74.

49. 6.7-12.

50. 7.273-78.

51. 7.712.

52. This has been dealt with above in the material superscribed to references nos. 8 and 9 of this chapter.

53. Stein, op. cit., Introduction, vol. I, p. 20.

54. In the references which follow, the first entry will be keyed to the Sanskrit text as edited by Jagadīś Lāl Śāstrī (Delhi: 1970); the second entry, labelled T-P, will be keyed to *The Ocean of Story*, trans., C.H. Tawney, ed., N.M. Penzer (reprinted: Delhi, 1968).

55. E.g., 13.54ff. T-P vol. I, pp. 156ff.

56. 122.20ff. T-P vol. IX, pp. 36ff.

57. 30.91-137. T-P vol. III, pp. 70-74.

58. 33.133-56. T-P vol. III, pp. 118-20.

59. 27.123-31. T-P vol. III, pp. 10-11.

60. 56.4ff. T-P vol. III, pp. 220ff.

61. 56.13. T-P vol. III, pp. 220-21.

62. 72.204-15. T-P vol. VI, pp. 83-84.

63. 38.47-72. T-P vol. III, pp. 209-11. Almost identical is 98.69-75; 99.1-41. T-P vol. VII, pp. 120-25. The "show-me-first' motif is found here also.

64. 26.193-255. T-P vol. II, pp. 231-36.

65. 15.30-53. T-P vol. II, pp. 4-5.

66. References will be to Johannes Hertel's edition of the Sanskrit text, entitled *The Thirty-two Bharaṭaka Stories*, No. 2 in the series of the Forschungsinstitut Für Indogermanistik Indische Abteilung, Sächsische Forschungsinstitute in Leipzig (Leipzig: 1921).

67. Introduction, p. 7.

68. The text offers no explanation of this occurrence.

69. Tale No. 2, pp. 22-23.

70. Tale No. 4, p. 26.

71. Tale No. 12, p. 31.

72. Tale No. 16, p. 34.

73. Tale No. 19. p. 35.

Chapter 4

THE BHĀṆA AND PRAHASANA LITERATURE

One-act monologue plays (*bhāṇas*) and farces (*prahasanas*) in Sanskrit have to this date received relatively little attention from scholars. The reason for their comparative neglect is most probably their oft-asserted vulgarity. Nevertheless, the strong current of satire and social criticism which runs through these plays makes their inclusion in this essay mandatory. As social criticism and satire are found at their sharpest in the earliest surviving specimens of this genre, it is primarily these which will be studied here.

Definitions

If we follow generally the rules laid down by Bharata in the fourth or the fifth century A.D., we find that a *bhāṇa* is a monologue spoken by a dissolute hero called *viṭa*. Dialogue is simulated by having the *viṭa* respond to imagined voices or asking questions of unseen characters and repeating their answers to the audience, saying 'What do you say?' and so on. As the action of the play takes the hero through streets lined with brothels and gambling dens, its movement has been described by S.K. De as a 'Rake's Progress.' Yet, the allusion to Hogarth's paintings should not be presssed too far: in the *bhāṇa*, the rake always happily accomplishes his mission and closes his monologue with a description of twilight setting on a successful day. We are able to induce something about the development of the *bhāṇa* if we return to Bharata and note both his advice that a play of this type should contain elements of a kind of dance called the *lāsya* and his prescription of the graceful style, or *kaiśikī vṛtti*, which allows for love and gallantry. As no surviving *bhāṇa* contains any elements of *lāsya* to speak of, we must conclude that this feature may well have characterized early *bhāṇas*, but fell into disuse as their composition became less popular and more literary in appeal. At the close of the tenth century, Dhanañjaya specified that a *bhāṇa* should be rendered in the *bhāratī vṛtti* and that the heroic (*vīra*) and erotic (*śṛṅgāra*) sentiments should prevail. Even the earliest surviving *bhāṇas* contain elements of studied elegance and humour which rule out the fostering of the heroic sentiment. That such elegance—especially in the creation of the erotic or *śṛṅgāra* sentiment—should gradually supersede even the satiric impulse, explains why we must turn to the earliest *bhāṇas* for anything more than nominal social criticism. Strangely, neither Bharata nor Dhanañjaya make specific mention of the comic element. However, in his comment on Bharata's text, Abhinavagupta observes that characters like the *viṭa* and his acquaintances are humorous and that *bhāṇa* and *prahasana* have a similar function and aim (*samānayoga-kṣema*). Dhanañjaya's prescription of the *bhāratī vṛtti*, moreover, perhaps *suggests* the comic element through the association of that style with the *prahasana*. It is most interesting to note that a still later theorist, Viśvanātha, explains Dhanañjaya's prescription of the *bhāratī vṛtti* as allowing occasional employment of the *kaiśikī vṛtti* specifically forbidden by Bharata. Since the *kaiśikī vṛtti* does give scope for love, gallantry and coquetry, it is tempting to see in this reversal of rules a corresponding shift in dramatic composition over the centuries between Bharata and Viśvanātha, favouring *śṛṅgāra* to the detriment of satire. It should not then be surprising that the liveliest satire and most effective social criticism should be found in a group of *bhāṇas* generally regarded as representing the earliest surviving specimens of the genre.[1] As this group of early *bhāṇas* was at first and subsequently published collectively, it has become conventional to refer to all four as the *Caturbhāṇī*.

The Character of the Caturbhāṇī

By *Caturbhāṇī*, the following four plays are meant: the *Padma-prābhṛtaka* (*Pp*), ascribed to Śūdraka; the *Ubhayābhisārikā* (*Ubh*), ascribed to Vararuci; the *Dhūrta-viṭa-saṃvāda* (*Dvs*), ascribed to Īśvaradatta; and, the *Pādatāḍitaka* (*Pt*), ascribed to Śyāmilaka. Of these, A. B. Keith wrote that 'no reliance can be placed on the first two ascriptions, and none of the plays need be older than 1000 A.D.'[2] Leaving aside the accuracy of the ascriptions, several scholars have since argued that the *Caturbhāṇī* are of a somewhat earlier time, perhaps as early as the Gupta era. M. Ramakrishna Kavi and S. K. Ramanatha Sastri, the two scholars who first edited and published the plays, claimed a great antiquity for their discoveries. A note of compromise was struck by F. W. Thomas, who found 'lexicographical and stylistic affinities to Bāṇa'[3] in the fourth play (*Pt*), and suggested for this reason that an approximate date of about the sixth or seventh centuries might be reasonable. Thomas sought to bolster his argument by suggesting that the splendid description of the city of Pāṭalīputra in the *Ubh* could only have been composed before that city entered into a long period of decline after the seventh century A.D.[4] But, whether or not the description of Pāṭalīputra in the *Ubh* is accurate, the four *bhāṇas* given locations in cities of the north and west clearly sets them apart from their successors, which are all set in the south.[5] But, most importantly, it is the quality of their satire and, beyond even that, their style, treatment and general atmosphere which distinguish the *Caturbhāṇī*.

Satiric Elements in the Caturbhāṇī

The action of the *Padma-prābhṛtaka* (*Pp*) finds the *viṭa* traversing the streets of Ujjayinī in the role of go-between for his friend, the legendary rascal Karṇīputra Mūladeva, who wishes the *viṭa* to determine the feelings his beloved prostitute, Devasenā, Mūladeva's suit is complicated by the fact that he has long been the lover of Devasenā's sister, Devadattā. As is evident from their names, both women follow the same profession.[6] After encountering the usual number of characters on his way, the *viṭa* returns to Mūladeva, bearing a lotus (as a token of Devasenā's love, which gives the play its name).

Both Brāhmaṇas and Buddhists are lampooned in the course of the *viṭa*'s monologue. First, there is Dattakalaśi, a pedantic Pāṇinian grammarian who proclaims his learning with sesquipedalian locutions. When not quarrelling with the despised Kātantrikas, he finds time for some hypocritical debauchery. Next is Pavitraka, who, as his name suggests, affects great purity. He is the profligate son of a Dharmāsanika.[7] As sketched here, Pavitraka has the twin faults of prudishness and hypocrisy. More forceful is Śaiṣilaka, a dissolute young Brāhmaṇa, encountered as he emerges from a gambling den. He is portrayed as the rapist of a Buddhist nun. But any suspicions of the *Pp*'s author's possible pro-Buddhist sympathies are dispelled by his portrait of the monk Śaṅkhilaka. The *viṭa* catches a glimpse of

Śaṅkhilaka sneaking out of a brothel, attempting to conceal the ends of his ochre robe. The *viṭa* laments the fact that the purity of the Buddha's teaching is defiled daily by such hypocrites who are esteemed by ordinary mortals. When stopped by the *viṭa*'s abusive greeting, the monk offers the excuse that he has only come to console the prostitute upon the loss of her mother. Rejecting this prevarication for what it is, the *viṭa*, with a fine simile, compares a monk's presence in a brothel to the prayer *Om* sanctimoniously prefixed to Dattaka's sexual *sūtras*. The *viṭa* closes this interview by seeking something to wash the defiling vision of the monk from his eyes.

The *Ubhayābhisārikā* (*Ubh*) shows its *viṭa* moving through the streets of Pāṭalīputra with the goal of mending a lovers' quarrel between a friend and his beloved prostitute. The most interesting character he encounters is Vilāsakauṇḍinī, a wandering Buddhist nun. Though she affects disinterest in anything other than high-flown Vaiśeṣika and Sāṅkhya philosophy, her appearance betrays her true devotion to affairs of the heart. Though she at first rebukes the *viṭa*'s cordial insinuations, she later confirms his suspicions with a laugh. Though the *Ubh* presents several other barbed depictions of Pāṭalīputra's residents, they concern mainly the machinations of prostitutes and so fall beyond the stated range of this essay. Of minor interest is the king's brother-in-law's involvement with prostitutes, including a fearfully domineering hag inappropriately named Sukumārikā.

The subject matter of the *Dhūrta-viṭa-samvāda* is somewhat different. This *bhāṇa* depicts a penniless *viṭa* who is too impoverished to indulge in his favourite pastimes of drinking and gambling. So, having nothing better to do, he wanders familiar brothel-lined streets to the house of his friends Viśvalaka and Sunandā. The former is an equally penniless, naked monk whose fondness for prostitutes has left him diseased and impotent. His mistress, Sunandā, is a shrivelled old wench with no other option but to remain at his side. The conversation mentioned in the play's title transpires between the *viṭa* and Viśvalaka. The talk centres upon questions of the conduct of affairs between prostitutes and their lovers, and so need not concern us here. Yet, Viśvalaka's reply to a question concerning the proper way to propitiate an offended prostitute does contain a noteworthy irreverence toward Brāhmaṇas. He declares that falling at the offended woman's feet is unimpressive, when it is customary to fall at the smelly, corn-studded feet of old *śrotriyas*.

At the beginning of the *Pāda-tāḍitaka* (*Pt*), the author clearly articulates his stance against hypocrisy:

> Depart, pray, you people of lives like cranes and cats,
> Respectable counsellors [*rājasaciva-s*], quietist pious folk:
> Stay, painters and poets and experts in frolic and arts;
> No flies with its honey the concourse of 'sharps' [*dhūrtas*] would drink.
> The hermit attains not by weeping his soul's release;
> Gay chatter is not to the prospect of heaven a bar:
> Then laugh, O ye wise, if ye please, and be easy of heart;
> Away with the solemn pretenses of pharisaism.[8]

The plot of the *Pt* (much the longest of the four *bhāṇas*) subjects the affectation of ritual purity to sustained satire. A foppish Brāhmaṇa youth named Viṣṇunāga has sought to assuage his beloved prostitute's pique by falling at her feet. Her reply was to honour his sacred crest-lock with a blow from her foot (a *pādatāḍitaka*). He responds with these words:

> This head, whose crest my mother with careful hand tied tight.
> Which my father kissed, as I bowed before him, saying 'a good boy',
> Which twice-born sprinkled with holy water and scraps of flowers,
> Your foot has been set upon it in pride, and my dignity slighted.[9]

Viṣṇunāga makes it clear that this incident has done more than merely injure his well-bred pride: the fact that a prostitute's lowly foot has touched such a sacred spot as his head has brought him to nothing less than a state of ritual defilement. The *viṭa*-narrator regards the young hypocrite as unworthy of so great an honour. Nevertheless, the next morning finds Viṣṇunāga explaining his misfortune before a panel of senior Brāhmaṇas, in the hope that they may recommend a suitable expiation (*prāyaścitta*) whereby he may regain his ritual purity. The Brāhmaṇas ill-contain their amusement over the young man's plight, but regretfully inform him that the books of Hindu law are silent on the proper means of expiating a grievous defilement of this sort. Hearing this bad news, Viṣṇunāga lifts up his hands and implores the elders not to abandon him as though he were a Śūdra:

> An Ārya am I; my life is pure, my family good;
> I have toiled at grammar and the rules of logic:
> A king's secretary am I and no common person:
> Help a pure man at his wits end. I am your suppliant.'
> At these words in that company—
> Some saying 'this is an ox', nudged one another with their elbows;
> 'A madman, perhaps', said some, and stood still and gazed at him long with smiling faces;
> 'Love-bewitched', said others, and cried out, putting a straw between him and them:
> Some again pitied the girl herself, saying, 'her sins have found her out.'[10]

At last, a solution is offered by a learned Brāhmaṇa wag. Noting that local custom and the judgement of one's peers take precedence on moot points of canon law, he advises Viṣṇunāga to convene an assembly of his fellow-rakes and expiate his sin in accordance with their advice.

We are given an amusing catalogue of rakes as the jury is selected. Included there is a humorous depiction of a hypocrite occurring when someone takes exception to the suggestion of a highly-placed man's name:

> What say you? 'As to all the rest, good. But Dayitaviṣṇu, is he approved by you as a rake?' No question. What say you? 'What, the king's half-brother, the poet, in command of the troops?' Certainly, precisely so. What say you? 'It can't be—
>
> 'The man, who despite the king's favour shrinks back,
> Who with ceremony (*maṅgala*) goes to his bed and gets up,

Who from worshipping the gods has his clothes all aroma'd
with bdellium,
And a triad of callosity hardening forehead and knees.'
'Moreover,
From temple to palace, from palace to temple he goes:
Thus in constant attendance on these two he passes his days.'
'He a rake!'[11]

This hypocrite is also proved to be a rake and the council is convened.

The presiding rake impresses his fellows with the seriousness of their duty, admonishing them that if they err they should be condemned to perpetual loss while gambling; to minding their mothers and showing deference to their fathers; to drinking boiled milk and watery sweets; and—worst of all—to getting married. So each member of the group addresses himself to Viṣṇunāga's dilemma responsibly. One proposes that the prostitute herself should seek an expiation for the defilement of touching her foot to the head of such an oaf. Another suggests that Viṣṇunāga can be dragged by her belt. Yet another suggests that he be lashed with her earring. Still one more suggests that Viṣṇunāga's head be washed with her foot-bath and that he should be required to drink the remainder. But, in the end, all resolve that Viṣṇunāga's holy head be forbidden the delicate touch of women's hands and that, as a consolation, the prostitute should place her foot on the chief rake's head in the sight of Viṣṇunāga!

The achievement of the authors of the *Caturbhāṇī* has been well-stated by F. W. Thomas. He finds that these plays 'have a real literary quality.' Moreover,

> They display a natural humour and a polite, intensely Indian irony which need not fear comparison with that of a Ben Jonson or a Moliere. The language is the veritable ambrosia of Sanskrit speech. Ordinarily we do not quite realize in what a degree the Sanskrit literature is a high literature of courts and serious circles, an observation which applies not only to learned treatises and to such works as Bāṇa's *Kādambarī*, but even to the *Daśa-kumāracarita* of Daṇḍin

and the polite drama. Here we have a good natural and easy Sanskrit (for Prākrit passages are very few) of a conversational tone, treating satirically of ordinary incidents and scandalous gossip. The writers claim to be poets and insert many well-turned verses, though they appeal to a particular audience.[12]

It is regrettable that later *bhāṇas* largely turned away from satire in favour of *śṛṅgāra*.[13] What little satire these later works contain comes incidentally in the form of brief descriptions of a licentious Paurāṇika, a preposterous old *śrotriya*, hypocritical or fraudulent Jaṅgamas, Śaivas, and Vaiṣṇavas. Bhāgavatas are ridiculed in Vatsarāja's *Hāsyacūḍāmaṇi*,[14] but, as S. K. De stresses, such satire 'is *not* a common feature'[15] of these works.

Prahasanas

The broader format of the Sanskrit farce, or *prahasana*, allows room for more satire than we find in the *bhāṇas*. Unfortunately, this potential was only imperfectly realized: the later *prahasanas* show the same tendency to strive less for the social criticism of satire and more for increasingly vulgar sexual humour. Again as with the *bhāṇas*, the earliest *prahasanas* suit our purposes best.

The Matta-vilāsa

The earliest known *prahasana* is the *Matta-vilāsa* of king Mahendravikrama of Kāñcī (about A.D. 620). As the play's title suggests, its action depicts the adventures of a drunken Śaiva mendicant (a skull-bearing Kapālin) in the streets of that South Indian city.

The first scene of the farce proper opens with the Kapālin, Satyasoma, staggering about in the company of his wench, Devasomā, also drunk. The state of the Kapālin's mind is indicated by the fact that he is unsure if his beloved's name is Devasomā or Somadevā. This error—which invites Devasomā's angry suspicion that she has a rival—causes the remorseful Kapālin to renounce liquor. However, he is easily dissuaded from this momentary vow when Devasomā falls at his feet, begging that he not forsake his holy practice (of habitual drunkenness), for her sake. The Kapālin consents and praises

Śiva, who found that salvation is earned with such practices. Moreover, he continues, so-called genuine ascetics are heretical sinners. Discovering a drinking establishment he declares that he finds there the splendour of a sacred sacrificial site: the liquor is the sacred Soma; the drinkers are the priests; the roasted meats are the fire-offerings; the drinkers' words are the text of the *Yajurveda*; their drunken song, the *Sāmaveda* chants; the bartender, the *yajamāna*!

Moving on, the Kapālin is about to accept some alms in his skull-bowl when he discovers that he has misplaced it. He determines that the precious object must have been stolen, and makes his sympathies clear by announcing that the villain must have been either a dog or a Buddhist monk. And, as luck would have it, a hapless Buddhist monk appears before him at that moment. The monk's character is revealed in his revery: he reflects with pleasure upon the meat and fish he has gained for alms, but wonders how it is that the all-knowing Buddha could have been so careless as to forget to sanction the enjoyment of liquor and women. He decides that the Buddha must not have been so forgetful, but rather that his remarks on this subject were doubtless expunged from the scriptures by villainous Elders, envious of younger monks' pleasures. He resolves to find an uncorrupted text to corroborate his hunch.

The Kapālin chases and catches the monk, who reacts indignantly, then falls to admiring Devasomā's beauty. After the three share a drink, the Kapālin becomes convinced once more that the Buddhist's concealed begging bowl is his lost skull-cap. A slapstick scuffle ensues, with Devasomā falling to the ground when she tries to grab onto the non-existent hair of the monk's shaven head.

A degenerate Pāśupata ascetic appears and offers to arbitrate the dispute, with a mind to winning Devasomā for himself.

When it is decided to take the matter to court, Devasomā gives her view of contemporary justice, lamenting that the Buddhist's connection with rich monasteries will permit him to stuff the mouths of the court officials. Just then, a madman is discovered wandering with the bowl in his hand. When the bowl is returned to the Kapālin, all concerned become fast friends and the farce comes to a close.[16]

As the above summary proves, the satire of the *Mattavilāsa* is caustic enough, but is not sufficiently incisive to rank as the best satire.

The Later Farces

Among the later farces, perhaps the most amusing is the *Bhagavad-ajjukīya*.[17] Its plot involves the exchange of souls between a genuine saint and a prostitute. Although its situation is humorous, there is little satire in the piece, let alone social criticism.

Among this group, the most relevant to our concern is the *Laṭaka-melaka* or 'Conference of Scoundrels' of Kavirāja Śaṅkhadhara (twelfth century). The conference of the title is called together by a procuress to determine who is best suited to win the favour of one Madanamañjarī. Although the characters of this farce are undeniably the limited representations of particular stock faults, their names are quite delightful. There are here the parasite Kulavyādhi (disease of his family); a shrewish wife Kalahapriyā (fond of discord); a Digambara monk Jaṭāsura (demon with matted hair); a Kāpālika, Ajñānaśri (rich in ignorance); hypocritical Brāhmaṇa Mithyāśukla (falsely pure); and a depraved Buddhist monk named Vyasanākara (ocean of vice). In the end, the old procuress herself marries the Digambara Jaina monk.[18]

As by this point the Sanskrit farce has come down to little more than caricatures, it should suffice to merely call attention to some of the names of a few of the characters we find there. Kings are named Anaya-sindhu (ocean of misrule), Kali-vatsala (strife's darling), and Duritārṇava (sea of misconduct). Their Brāhmaṇical counsellors are given names like Viśvabhāṇḍa (universal hypocrite), Dharmānala (consuming fire of law), and Anṛtasarvasva (sum total of falsehood).

The Prabodhacandrodaya

Though, strictly speaking, Kṛṣṇa Miśra's *Prabodhacandrodaya*[19] is neither a *bhāṇa* nor a *prahasana*, it does combine some humour with allegorical solemnity to present a fuller dramatic portrait of the kind of Kāpālika we have already seen lampooned in the *Matta-vilāsa*. It presents the personified Tranquillity in search of her lost mother, Faith. Representatives of the Jaina and Buddhist religions appear to persuade Tranquillity to find

Faith in their creeds. They are soon overshadowed by a Kāpālika, who displays his ornaments made of human bones and relates his practice of dwelling in cremation grounds, and eating his food and drinking his liquor from a Brāhmaṇa's skull. The Jaina monk repudiates these and other Kāpālika practices such as human sacrifice. But both the Jaina and the Buddhist convert quickly to the Kāpālika practice when they behold the Kāpālika's seductive Kāpālinī. They demur to accept the Kāpālika's offer of liquor, but are easily persuaded to forego their reticence when the Kāpālinī—Faith drinks first. It is clear that the heretics will undergo any extent of ritual pollution with sufficient inducement. In the end, True Faith joins forces with orthodox *Dharma* and Devotion to Viṣṇu. Although he admits that the account of the *Prabodhacandrodaya* is 'highly tendentious and distorted', the author of a recent book on Kāpālikas still finds that of all the literary sources of information on that sect this allegorical play 'is in many respects the most informative'.[20]

In conclusion, we find that the *bhāṇa* and *prahasana* literature are not lacking in social criticism expressed in satire and caricature. Nevertheless, it seems to this writer that the broad and farcial stereotypes it employs to these ends lack Daṇḍin's charm and Kṣemendra's incisive realism.

References

1. S.K. De, 'A Note on the Sanskrit Monologue-Play (Bhāṇa), with Special Reference to the Caturbhāṇī', *JRAS*, 1926, pp. 63-68.
2. A.B. Keith, *SD*, p. 185, n. 3.
3. *JRAS*, 1924, pp. 262-65.
4. Moticandra also accepted the Gupta era as the probable date for these plays. Cf. p. 87 of his Hindī introduction to his edn. of the *Caturbhāṇī* [the running title; the bookjacket reads *Śṛṅgār-Hāṭ*] which includes Hindī translations of the plays done in collaboration with V.S. Agrawala (Bombay: Hindī Granth Ratnākar Kāryālay Pvt. Ltd., 1959). De (op. cit., pp. 75-76, n. 1) notes that 'this [description of Pāṭalīputra], of course, is not conclusive, as such descriptions could have been conventional'; but adds, 'the description here, however, appears too vivid to be merely conventional.' For my part, I find the description too hyperbolic to be construed as the literal representation of the city at any time.
5. Even the *Pt*'s fictitious 'Sārvabhauma' seems like a cosmopolitan city of the West. Cf. De, op. cit., pp. 79-80.

6. The following is recorded in Bharata's *Nāṭya-śāstra: 'datta mitrā ca senāveśyānāmāni yojayet'* (*GOS*, 17.98)—cited by T. Venkatacharya and A.K. Warder, *The Ubhayābhisārikā or 'Both Go To Meet'* (Madras: V. Sambamurthy, 1967), p. 58, n. 6b.

7. Apparently a high magistrate.

8. Trans., F.W. Thomas, 'Four Sanskrit Plays', *JRAS, Centenary Supplement*, (Oct., 1924), p. 136. The text is found on pp. 150-51 of the Moticandra-Agrawala ed., op. cit.

9. Trans., Thomas, op. cit., p. 131.

10. Ibid., p. 132.

11. Ibid., p. 133.

12. Ibid., pp. 135-36.

13. Cf., De, op. cit., p. 84, where it is said that 'the very names of later *bhāṇas*, such as *Śṛṅgāra-bhūṣaṇa*, *Śṛṅgāra-tilaka*, *Śṛṅgāra-sarvasva*, *Śṛṅgāra-mañjarī*. . [etc.], emphasize their exclusive tendency towards the erotic and their diminishing interest in comedy or satire.'

14. Ed., Jayasankar Tripathi (Prayāga: Devabhāṣā Prakāśana, 1970-71).

15. Ibid., p. 72.

16. The text is published with the 'Prakāśa' Hindī commentary of Kapiladeva Giri as no. 135 in the *Vidyabhawan Sanskrit Granthamala* (Varanasi: Chowkhamba Vidyabhawan, 1966). Trans. into German by Johannes Hertel as *Die Streiche des Berauschten* (Leipzig: H. Haessel, 1924). Trans. into English by L.D. Barnett, *BSOS*, V, pt. 4 (1930), pp. 697-717.

17. Ed., Prabhakara Sastri Veturi (Madras: Vavilla Press, 1925).

18. Printed with the 'Prakāśa' Hindī commentary of Kapiladeva Giri as no. 87 in the *Vidyabhawan Sanskrit Granthamala* (Varanasi: Chowkhamba Vidyabhawan, 1962).

19. Ed. with 'Prakāśa' Sanskrit-Hindī commentaries by Ramacandra Misra as no. 14 in the *Vidyabhawan Sanskrit Granthamala* (Varanasi: Chowkhamba Vidyabhawan, 1968). Trans. J. Taylor, 2nd ed. (Bombay: Tookaram Tatya, 1893).

20. David N. Lorenzen, *The Kāpālikas and Kālāmukhas: Two Lost Śaivite Sects*, vol. XII of the *Australian National University Centre of Oriental Studies, Oriental Monograph Series* (New Delhi: Thomson Press Ltd., 1972), p. 62.

Chapter 5

DIVERSITY OF THOUGHT IN THE SUBHĀṢITA COLLECTIONS

The word *subhāṣita* literally means something well-said. As a literary term, it is used to denote the expression of any of an exceptionally broad range of thoughts within the compass of a single stanza. Given this very flexible format, *subhāṣitas* paint the world and its manifold aspects in brilliant miniatures; moreover, they often satirically puncture human pretensions, impart moral and ethical advice, or simply summarize what their authors believe every thinking person should know at a minimum about any given subject.[1]

Subhāṣitas are found in the oldest books of Sanskrit literature: in the first chapter above (p. 7), a *subhāṣita* was quoted from the *Aitareya Brāhmaṇa*. Similarly, *subhāṣitas* occur in the *Ṛgveda*, the *upaniṣads*, in the epics and *dharmaśāstras*. The oldest anthologies of verses by different authors are in Prākṛt: Hāla's *Sattasaī*, Jayavallabha's *Vajjālagga* and the Chapaṇṇaya *Gāhāo*.[2] The oldest anthologies in Sanskrit date from the eleventh to the fourteenth centuries A.D. These include the *Subhāṣitaratna-koṣa* of Vidyākara,[3] the *Saduktikarṇāmṛta*[4] (A.D. 1205) of Śrīdharadāsa, the *Sūktimuktāvali*[5] (A.D. 1258) of Jalhaṇa, the *Śārṅgadhara-paddharti*[6] (A.D. 1363) of Śārṅgadhara, and the *Subhāṣitasudhānidhi*[7] (first half of the fourteenth century A.D.). Once started, the compilation of anthologies of *subhāṣitas* in Sanskrit continued at a rate remarkable even in the history of Sanskrit literature, where one often encounters long lists of works in a given field. If one considers unpublished—and even *unregistered*—manuscripts, the number of surviving *subhāṣita* collections must be in the hundreds. And this refers only to the anthologies taken as a whole; the number of verses they contain is surely staggering. While it is true that many smaller anthologies may contain only one, two or three hundred stanzas, it is also true that others contain thousands. As we come to the anthologies put together in our time, the size of these collections seems to be still growing. One particularly well-chosen collection published (in its eighth edition) twenty-five years ago had grown to include more than 11,000 verses, many of exceptional quality.[8] As significant an achievement as this doubtless is, it pales before the most recent *subhāṣita* project: Ludwik Sternbach is currently involved in the herculean task of collecting and publishing a projected 50-60,000 descriptive and ethical *subhāṣitas* in a *Mahā-subhāṣitasaṅgraha* running to more than twenty volumes. Considering the vast amount of verses to be collected and studied, it is small wonder that the cultural material they contain has only begun to be exploited. Thus it is with perfect justification that Sternbach remarks that the *subhāṣita-saṅgrahas* form 'a forgotten chapter in the histories of Sanskrit literature.'[9]

But what is it in the *subhāṣita-saṅgrahas* which make combing through them worthwhile? To begin with, these anthologies contain thought similar to that found in other branches of Sanskrit literature, but 'ne'er so well express'. But, beyond that, *subhāṣitas* often move beyond the idealized, fanciful world of *kāvyas* and *purāṇas* to show us how ordinary people lived and thought in India's past. It is this fact which best explains the perennial buoyancy of *subhāṣitas* within oral tradition. As Sternbach says, the anthologies 'are storehouses of information about the life of the common people of India between the eleventh and nineteenth century. This information, easily available in these collections, can only be found there, since the other sources of Indian literature describe rather the life of kings, Brāhmaṇa-s and nobles.'[10] It has been the purpose of the above four chapters to show that such information as that which Sternbach claims is exclusively available in the anthologies *is* available elsewhere; nevertheless, his statement does properly emphasize the importance of these collections to any thorough study of such material.

The Common Touch

The *kāvyas* are filled with princes encountering extraordinarily beautiful princesses in pleasure-gardens or in palaces with fountains, jewel-studded walls and opalescent floors. The following *subhāṣita*'s depiction of the householder's life will serve to contrast such an atmosphere with the much more mundane world of the *anthologies*:

krośantaḥ śiśavaḥ savāri sadanaṃ paṅkāvṛtaṃ cāṅgaṇaṃ
śāyyā daṃśavatī ca rūkṣamaśanaṃ dhūmena pūrṇaṃ gṛham //
bhāryā niṣṭhurabhāṣiṇī prabhurapi krodhena pūrṇaḥ sadā
snānaṃ śītalavāriṇā hi satataṃ dhigdhiggṛhasthāśramam //[11]

Bawling kids, a damp seat, a courtyard covered with mud, a bed filled with biting insects, dried-up food, a house filled with smoke [from the hearth], a sharp-tongued wife, an angry husband, and always a cold-water bath—Damn forever the householder's life!

Living in another's house and depending on that person's charity is no better: a second verse observes that the moon is carried by Śiva himself, but even that blessing cannot prevent its waning.[12]

As the last verse shows, *subhāṣitas* often have a moral or ethical tone. The following verse on ingratitude is even more strongly didactic:

brahmaghne ca surāpe ca core bhagnavrate tathā /
niṣkṛtirvihitā loke kṛtaghne nāsti niṣkṛtiḥ //[13]

Expiation is laid down for a Brāhmaṇa-killer, a drinker, a thief, and a vow-breaker. But, for an ungrateful person there is no expiation in the world.

Though often moral, *subhāṣitas* consistently commend practical virtues over the asceticism romanticized in the epics and Purāṇas.

ahiṃsā satyavacanamanṛśaṃsyaṃ damo ghṛṇā /
etattapo vidurdhīrā na śarīrasya śoṣaṇam //[14]

True asceticism lies not in the emaciation of one's body, but rather in non-violence, truthfulness, gentility, restraint and compassion. Another verse tells us that the ascetic's forest retreat has its pitfalls and that it is better to look for virtue in an honest labourer's house.[15] Another verse compares ascetics who angrily teach others not to lose their tempers with penniless alchemists teaching others the secret of becoming rich.[16] In contrast with the pusillanimous 'renunciation' of some ascetics, consider the lovely humanistic spirit which pervades the following verse:

ye tāvatsvaguṇopabṛṃhitadhiyasteṣāmaraṇyaṃjagadye'pyete
kṛtamatsarāḥ paraguṇaṃ svapne'pi necchanti ye /

anyeṣāmanurāgiṇāṃ kvacidapi snigdhaṃ mano nirvṛtāvitthaṃ
yāntu tapovanāni mahatāṃ sūktāni manye' dhunā //[17]

There are those whose minds are so puffed up with their own virtue that for them their penance forest is no better than the world. They are so maliciously envious that they would not care to suffer another's virtue even in a dream.

There are other, passionate people whose affectionate minds find beatitude anywhere. Let them go on: I now find penance forests in well-expressed thoughts of the great.

Scoundrels: Quacks, Astrologers and Bureaucrats

The *subhāṣita* collections reveal a regard for quack physicians, astrologers and Kāyastha bureaucrats similar to that of Kṣemendra. The following verse, attributed to Maya, could well have been composed by Kṣemendra:

vaidyanātha namastubhyaṃ kṣapitāśeṣamānava /
tvayi sannyastabhāro'yaṃ kṛtāntaḥ sukhamedhate //[18]

Hail to thee, Great Physician, who lays waste all mankind!
Having put his burden on thee, the God of Death flourishes happily!

There are many such verses which stress the quack's close association with the God of Death. One of them declares them brothers, but adds that while the God of death only takes one's life away, the physician takes both life and money.[19] Another verse observes that even such parasites as actors, astrologers and even Pāśupata ascetics will, when asked, give something. But how, it asks, can a physician, whose only thought is to plunder and kill, give anything?[20]

The anthologies depict astrologers as no better than whores[21] and only interested in filling their bellies.[22] One verse knowingly tells how astrologers hedge their predictions. First, they draw up the horoscope and forecast what good or ill will come to pass. If the predictions come true, then he proclaims his own acumen; if not, he looks again to see what was in the ascendant.[23] Or, declaring that all events were fated to occur, he always claims prior knowledge.[24]

The anthologies often include Kṣemendra's verses condemning Kāyastha bureaucrats. Other anonymous verses prove that Kṣemendra was probably not alone in resenting the abuses of this group. All verses emphasize the ruthlessness of the bureaucrats. The following verse, for example, provides a bitter etymology for the term 'Kāyastha':

> *kākāllaulyaṃ yamātkrauryaṃ sthapaternityaghātitām /*
> *ādyākṣarāṇi saṅgṛhya kāyasthaḥ kena nirmitaḥ //*[25]
> Taking greediness from the crow, cruelty from Death, perpetual oppression from kings and the first syllable from each [kā-ya-stha], who fashioned the Kāyastha?

Several verses demonstrate the Kāyastha bureaucrats' rapacity by affirming their taste for taboo foods. Such is the case in the next verse which gives the same sort of etymology for the term *divira* or official:

> *vinā madyaṃ vinā māṃsaṃ parasvaharuṇaṃ vinā /*
> *vinā parāpavādena diviro divi roditi //*[26]
> Without liquor, meat without taking away other's property, and without slander, bureaucrat howls to the heavens!

Another oft-quoted verse asserts that the only reason the Kāyastha in the womb does not eat his mother's entrails is because he fears they might not be meat (this explains his toothlessness).[27] As we see, the *subhāṣita* collections do not hesitate to include disgusting imagery. Such instances, however, are infrequent; this fact may serve as an indication of the contempt felt towards bureaucrats. Still another verse denies that a bureaucrat (—a *niyogī* this time—) drinks liquor and eats meat; instead, it says, he drinks the blood of good men from their throats![28]

Pāṇḍityam

The anthologies also voice criticism of the learnedness of *paṇḍitas*. A common theme is the emptiness of pedantry without practical wisdom. This is the message of our first verse:

> *yasya nāsti vivekastu kevalaṃ yo bahuśrutaḥ /*
> *na sa jānāti śāstrārthāndarvī pākarasāniva //*[29]
> One who, lacking discrimination, only learns much, [simply]

misses the point of the *śāstras*: as a ladle never tastes cooked food.

Another verse asserts that *śāstras,* though intended to impart gentility, only intoxicate inferior men with pride in the same way that owls are blinded by light.[30] And one more verse says that as a mirror is useless to one without eyes, so *śāstras* are of no use to one lacking innate wisdom.[31]

Such criticisms are also directed against *paṇḍitas* in the various fields of vedic study, Mīmāṃsā, logic and grammar. The following verse characterizes the time-serving, vedic teacher:

āḥ kaṣṭamaprahṛṣṭāḥ śiṣṭā api vittacāpalāviṣṭāḥ |
adhyāpayanti vedānādāya cirāya māsi māsi bhṛtim ||[32]
Alas! Though educated, they are bored and obsessed with money: taking their wages month after month, they teach the *Vedas*! for long.

Mīmāṃsakas are criticized along predictable lines: they are accused of losing the clear Vedic vision amidst the maze of their own pedantry. The two following verses typify these complaints:

te mīmāṃsāśāstralokaprasiddhāḥ sarvarṣīṇāṃ sehire naiva sattām |
caitanyasyāpahnavaṃ devatānāṃ cakrurviśvaṃ naśvaram manyamānāḥ ||[33]
Those celebrated in the world of *Mīmāṃsā-śāstras* have no tolerance for the truth of all the *ṛṣis*. They obscure the thought of the [very] gods and are considered a universal bane.
mīmāṃsakāḥ katicidatra milanti vedaprāmāṇyasādhanakṛto 'pi na te'bhivandyāḥ |
udghoṣito' pyupaniṣadbhiraśeṣaśeṣī brahmaiva nābhyupagataḥ puruṣottamo yaiḥ ||[34]
Even though *Mīmāṃsakas* gather together some material here in this world and devise means of securing Vedic authority, they none the less deserve no praise: they do not even approach the ultimate person proclaimed in the *upaniṣads*—Brāhmaṇa![35]

The next two verses proclaim the purposelessness of logicians' pedantry:

karmabrahmavicāraṇāṃ vijahato bhogāpavargapradāṃ, ghoṣaṃ kañcana kaṇṭhaśoṣaphalakaṃ kurvantyamī tārkikāḥ /
pratyakṣaṃ na punāti nāpaharate pāpāni pīlucchaṭāvyāptirnāvati naiva pātyanumitirno pakṣatā rakṣati //[36]

These logicians put aside thoughts of *karma* and Brahman—which impart satisfaction and liberation—and grow hoarse proclaiming some [doctrine or another]. *Pratyakṣa* (visible evidence) neither increases nor abets sin; the universal pervasion of atoms (*pīlucchaṭavyāpti*) offers no refuge; neither does inference and defending a proposition!

sādhu vyākaraṇaṃ hitāya viśadaṃ kāvyaṃ pikīgītavan-mīmāṃsā śrutitatparā tadanugaṃ sāṅkhyaṃ sapātañjalam /
tvaṃ tu nyāya viśuddhavaidikavidhivyākopabauddhāgamavyāghātāya nigūḍhatarkagahana kvāmodamādhāsyasi //[37]

Excellent grammar is beneficial; poetry is as lovely as a female cuckoo's song; Mīmāṃsā, Sāṅkhya and Pātañjala Yoga are devoted to revealed texts. But you, O Logic, Impenetrable through Obscure Argumentation, are dedicated to assailing Buddhist scriptures and contradicting the pure Vedic way. What comfort do you give?

The next verse has a logician condemn himself:

he he mitra jitā mayātibalino viprā dhanaṃ cārjitaṃ śeṣebhyaḥ śarayantradānamapi satsaṃpāditaṃ bhūriśaḥ /
granthāścāpi kṛtāḥ sutarkaghaṭakāḥ śāstrāṇi sandūṣya vai so 'ham tarkavibhūṣaṇo'tra gahane dhātrā sṛgālaḥ kṛtaḥ //[38]

O Friend! I have defeated formidable Brāhmaṇas, earned a fortune from the rest, and have elaborated voluminously the truth given in texts. I have also composed books of excellent dialectics and have refuted the śāstras. Indeed, I am the very ornament of disputation: a Brahmā-created jackal in the wild!

The pedantry of grammarians is also condemned as useless:

sūtraiḥ pāṇininirmitairbahutarairniṣpādya śabdāvaliṃ vaikuṇṭhastavamakṣamā racayituṃ mithyāśramāḥ śābdikāḥ /
pakvānnaṃ vividhaṃ śrameṇa vividhāpūpāgryasūpānvitaṃ mandāgnīnanurundhate mitabalānāghrātumapyakṣamān //[39]

Having readied declensional paradigms with the aid of enormous numbers of Pāṇinian *sūtras,* the hapless grammarians cannot compose a [simple] hymn to Viṣṇu!
They imitate emaciated dyspeptics who, after strenuously preparing an elaborate banquet replete with cakes and condiments, are unable to enjoy it.

Blissful Ignorance

Lest it be thought that *subhāṣitas* are rigidly anti-intellectual, a few verses condemning ignorance will now be quoted. The first verse is attributed to Udbhaṭa, who lived at the beginning of the ninth century.

mūrkhatvaṃ sulabhaṃ bhajasva kumate mūrkhasya cāṣṭau guṇā, niścinto bahubhojano'timukharo rātrindivaṃ svapnabhāk| kāryākāryavicāraṇāndhabadhiro mānāpamāne samaḥ, prāyeṇāmayavarjito dṛḍhavapurmūrkhaḥ sukhaṃ jīvati ||[40]
Go ahead, Blockhead, enjoy your easy stupidity!
The qualities of a fool are eightfold:
He is careless, gluttonous, garrulous, dreams day and night, is blind and deaf to the thought of what should and should not be done, is indifferent to honour and notoriety, and is generally fat and happy. The fool leads a comfortable existence.

Other verses announce that learning is wasted on a dunce.[41] Another verse has the theme that a little learning is a dangerous thing. It depicts those who take pride in their understanding of poetry without knowing the virtue of modestly concealing their expertise. The verse declares that such braggarts begin to taste the dread Hālāhala poison without having learned the antidote (Gāruḍīya *mantras*).[42] Our last verse declares it better to be a learned pauper than a rich dunce:

varaṃ daridraḥ śrutiśāstrapārago,
na cāpi mūrkho bahuratnasaṃyutaḥ |
sulocanā jīrṇapaṭāpi śobhate,
na netrahīnā kanakairalaṅkṛtā ||[43]

It is better to be a pauper with a command of *sāstras* and the scriptures than a fool bedecked with jewels. A woman with lovely eyes is radiant even in a tattered garment, but not an eyeless [hag] festooned with gold.

Noble Descent

Some of the criticisms collected in the *subhāṣita-saṅgrahas* were anticipated in the didactic writings of Kṣemendra. His *Darpadalana*, for example, examines pride of learning in its third section. Pride of noble birth is also considered in the first section of the same work. There Kṣemendra first offers some didactic verses warning against the pitfalls of such pride and afterwards illustrates his theme with a story of a haughty young Brāhmaṇa who discovers to his sorrow that his own pride of pure and noble descent is ill-founded. Several *subhāṣitas* of the sort considered just above emphasize the uselessness of noble descent in the case of the uneducated. The following two verses exemplify this theme:

> *rūpayauvanasampannā viśālakulasambhavāḥ |*
> *vidyāhīnā na śobhante nirgandhāḥ kiṃśukā iva ||*[44]
> Handsome and youthful men of great descent who still lack learning never shine; [they disappoint] like Kiṃśuka blossoms with no fragrance.
> *vidyāvidhivihīnena kiṃ kulīnena dehinām |*
> *akulīno'pi yo vidvāndaivatairapi pājyate ||*[45]
> What use among men is there for a well-bread man without learning and proper conduct? But even the gods revere a learned man of undistinguished origin.

Other verses[46] do not mention learning specifically, but stress conduct as the sole standard of a man's worth. The following example was chosen for its presumed antiquity:

> *na kulaṃ vṛttahīnānāṃ pramāṇamiti me matiḥ |*
> *anyeṣvapi hi jātānāṃ vṛttameva viśiṣyate ||*[47]
> In my opinion, distinguished birth is no standard [for judging] those deficient in conduct: for among those of other origins, conduct alone is singled out.

Our last verse on this subject is also the best. Though it is included in at least one *subhāṣita-saṅgraha*,[48] it can be traced to Kṛṣṇa-miśra's allegorical *Prabodhacandrodaya.*[49] Though shorter, it bears comparison with any of Browning's dramatic monologues. The speaker is Ego personified:

nāsmākaṃ jananī tathojjvalakulā sacchrotriyāṇāṃ kulādūḍhā
kācana kanyakā khalu mayā tenāsmi tātādhikaḥ |
asmatsyālakabhāgineyabhaginī mithyābhiśastā paraistatsam-
bandhavaśānmayā svagṛhiṇī preyasyapi projjhitā ||[50]

I married a maiden from a clan of true śrotriyas; my own mother was not so well-bred: therefore, I bettered myself in that respect. [But,] my brother-in-law's sister's son's sister was falsely defamed by enemies. On the strength of that, I put aside my wife in favour of one still better!

Undeserved Success

There is little doubt that verses such as those quoted above reflect a social conscience at work in the minds of the poets who composed them. But often, as in the following verses bemoaning the success of unqualified men, it is impossible to determine if the authors were motivated by popular outrage or the patrician contempt of a Coriolanus for the incompetent's elevation by the mob. Much of the problem, of course, stems from the tendency of the *saṅgrahas* to quote anonymous verses which we are unable to place in context. The next verse is a case in point:

uccairuccaritavyaṃ yatkiṃcidajānatāpi puruṣeṇa |
mūrkhā bahumanyante viduṣāmapi saṃśayo bhavati ||[51]

Fools think highly of whatever even an ignorant man proclaims loudly; the wise, however, have doubt.

Now with this verse we are left wondering whether its author meant to condemn the wealthy's patronage of aggressive incompetents, or demagogic pandering to the masses' sympathies, or something else entirely. The verse contrasts the ignorant with the wise, but is education really at issue here? In the next verse, thankfully, we may be sure that education *is* at issue:

mīmāṃsā paṭhitā na yairupaniṣannaiva śrutā tattvataḥ
śrīmacchaṅkarabhāṣyato bhagavatī gītāpyadhītā na yaiḥ |

siddhāntāpagataṃ śiromaṇimataṃ jñātvā' pi kiṃcittato,
bhaṭṭācāryapadaṃ gatāḥ kathamaho lajjāṃ labhante na te //[52]
There are those who have not read Mīmāṃsā; nor, truly, heard a single Upaniṣad, let alone studied even the *Bhagavadgītā* from Śaṅkara's commentary. But, working up something considered totally unfounded in the opinion of great scholars, they are then elevated to the position of great teachers: how is it they do not come to shame?

Serving the Rich and Powerful

It would perhaps be justified to see more popular sentiment in complaints relating to the service of the rich and powerful. The *saṅgrahas* contain a very substantial number of verses on this theme. Moreover, it is important to note that for a literature supposedly cultivated in response to royal patronage, its *subhāṣitas* voice frequent complaints *against* such patronage and against incompetent rulers in general. *Subhāṣitas* relating specifically to the patronage of poets will be treated at the conclusion of this essay.

Our first verse complains generally about the unfeeling indifference of the rich:

lakṣmīvanto na jānanti prāyeṇa paravedanām /
śeṣe dharābharaklānte śete nārāyaṇaḥ sukham //[53]
The rich generally do not perceive others' discomfort: Viṣṇu sleeps comfortably on Śeṣa, who is already wearied by the burden of the Earth.

The next verse is on the ill-manneredness of the rich:

bhakte dveṣo jaḍe prītiarucirgurulaṅghanam /
mukhe ca kaṭutā nityaṃ dhanināṃ jvariṇāmiva //[54]

Wading through the paranomasias, we find that this verse declares that even as a fever victim has an aversion to food, craves water,[55] is disinclined to fast, and always has a bitter taste in his mouth; even so, a rich man, hates his servant, is affectionate to fools, disrespects his elders and always has something caustic to say. It is admittedly difficult to regard a verse of such intricacy as a battle cry in a social revolution; nevertheless, the sympathies of its author are clear enough. The next verse has as its theme the dependency of the rich on their less fortunate servants:

> *āliṅgitāḥ parairyānti praskhalanti same pathi |*
> *avyaktāni ca bhāṣante dhanino madyapā iva ||*[56]
> [Though] they move supported by others, they trip on a smooth path and say unspeakable things—the wealthy are like drunkards.

Another verse associates such dependency with ingratitude:

> *ājanmānugate 'pyasminnāle vimukhamambujam |*
> *prāyeṇa guṇapūrṇeṣu rītirlakṣmīvatāmiyam ||*[57]
> A lotus with its face turned away from the stalk which has supported it from birth: this is the wealthy's general mode of behaviour with respect to the wholly virtuous.

The next verse seems to be a complaint against the capricious patronage of what is presumably a king (indicated by a white parasol):

> *peṭīcīvarapaṭṭavastrapaṭalaśvetātapatracchaṭāśāṭīhārakaghoṭa-kasphuṭaghaṭāṭopāya tubhyaṃ namaḥ |*
> *yenānakṣarakukṣayo'pi jagataḥ kurvanti sarvajñatābhrāntiṃ*
> *yena vinā tu hāsyapadavīṃ santo'pi kaṣṭaṃ gatāḥ ||*[58]

The verse hails an obviously wealthy patron replete, like a bursting pot, with such paraphernalia as baskets (*peṭī*), *cīvara* cloth, woven silks, numerous white parasols, *śāṭī* cloth, pearl necklaces and horses. It complains that through this patron the unlettered foist the false impression of omniscience upon the world, but allows that without such patronage even the best men would come to be ridiculed.

The next two verses are directed against princes:

> *paraparivādena guṇo veṣaviśeṣeṇa pauruṣātiśayaḥ*
> *yatkiṃcanakāritayā nṛṇāṃ bhavedrājaputratvam ||*[59]
> [Wherever] virtue is defined by the censure of others and manly excellence through distinction of dress and unpaid bills, [there] men have princely status.

chandorahitā gāthāḥ ślokānapaśabdaviṣadharagrastān |
paṭhato'pyaho sumahatī mahārghatā rājaputrasya ||[60]
Reciting *gāthās* without metre and *ślokas* bitten by the poisonous snakes of bad grammar: O what tremendous value has the son of a king!

Many verses decry a life of service to such people. The next verse speaks of serving the ignorant in a series of *dṛṣṭāntas* reflecting the utter futility of such a career:

araṇyaruditaṃ kṛtam śavaśarīramudvartitaṃ sthale'bjamavaropiṭam suciramūṣare varṣitam |
śvapucchamavanāmitaṃ badhirakarṇajāpaḥ kṛto dhṛto'ndhamukhadarpaṇo yadabudho janaḥ sevitaḥ ||[61]
Crying in the wilderness, beautifying a corpse, cultivating a lotus in the desert, a long rain on saline soil, holding a dog's tail down, speaking in a deaf man's ear, holding a mirror to a blind man's face—such is serving an ignorant man.

Two verses deal with the difficulty of serving a fickle master:

vijñaiḥ snigdhairupakṛtamapi dveṣatāmeti kaścit
sākṣādanyairapakṛtamapi prītimevopayāti |
citraṃ citraṃ kimatha caritaṃ naikabhāvāśrayāṇāṃ
sevādharmaḥ paramagahano yogināmapyagamyaḥ ||[62]
Even a favour done by skilful and affectionate men becomes an act of hostility. Even a hostile act done openly by others is deemed a favour—how surpassingly strange is the behaviour of the fickle-minded! Even the wise cannot fathom a servant's duty.

The second verse is noteworthy in that its target is a fickle king:

bhaktānāmupakāriṇāṃ parahitavyāpārayuktātmanāṃ
sevāsaṃvyavahāratattvaviḍusāṃ drohacyutānāmapi |
vyāpattiḥ skhalitāntareṣu niyatā siddhirbhavedvā na vā
tasmādambupaterivāvanipateḥ sevā sadāśaṅkanī ||[63]

This verse bears the gloomy message that successful or not, good servants come to inevitable ruin, even though they may be devoted, helpful, dedicated to the welfare of others, masterful in their service, and uncomplaining. Thus, the poet concludes, the service of kings, like dealing with the ocean, is a fearful matter.

One last verse speaks in general terms of the degradation inherent in servitude:

> *manuṣyajātau tulyāyāṃ bhṛtyatvamatigarhitam* /
> *prathamo yo na tatrāpi sa kiṃ jīvatsu gaṇyate* //[64]
> Mankind being equal, servitude is highly censurable. He who is not the first even there, can he be counted among the living?

Poverty

Even Kosambi grudgingly noted the sensitivity of verses on poverty in Vidyākara's *Subhāṣitaratnakoṣa*. Even then, he finds such verses to be too few. Yet, if these verses are taken together with many others of their kind in other *saṅgrahas*, the total gives impressive testimony to the social conscience of a good many Sanskrit poets. The sample verses quoted below (all from other anthologies) should bear this out.

Consider the sympathy which puts these words in a poor man's mouth:

> *kiṃ karomi kva gacchāmi kamupaimi durātmanā* /
> *durbhareṇodareṇāhaṃ prāṇairapi viḍambitaḥ* //[65]
> What may I do? Where may I go? To whom may I turn? My breath, burdensome belly, and wretched self all mock me.

Similarly,

> *dharmārthakāmahīnasya parakīyānnabhojinaḥ* /
> *kākasyeva daridrasya dīrghamāyurviḍambanā* //[66]
> A long life is a mockery for a poor man shorn of Dharma, Artha and Kāma and habituated to eating others' food—like a crow.

Several verses in the *saṅgrahas* echo the *Pañcatantra*'s depiction of the poor taking on a kind of invisibility as their more fortunate fellows increasingly ignore them. One such verse is as follows:

he dāridrya namastubhyaṃ siddho'haṃ tvatprasādataḥ |
paśyāmyahaṃ jagatsarvaṃ na māṃ paśyati kaścana ||[67]
O Poverty, hail to thee! By your grace I have attained supernatural powers: I see the whole world, but no one sees me!

The next verse is on the subject of fair-weather friends:

iha loke hi dhanināṃ paro'pi svajanāyate |
svajano'pi daridrāṇāṃ tatkṣaṇāddurjanāyate ||[68]
In this world, even an enemy becomes a kinsman to the wealthy. But, for the impoverished, a kinsman becomes instantly inimical.

Other verses describe the physical and psychological effects of poverty:

kaṇṭhe gadgadatā svedo mukhe vaivarṇyavepathū |
mriyamāṇasya cihnāni yāni tānyeva yācataḥ ||[69]
Stammering in the throat, perspiration on the face, pallor and trembling: one seeking alms has the exact symptoms of a dying man.

A note of class distinction is introduced in a similar verse which has the stammering occur in the throat of a well-bred man seeking money but ashamed to ask for it.[70] As the next verse shows, such men are ill-suited to survive hardship:

jīvantyarthakṣaye nīcā yācñopadravavañcanaiḥ |
kulābhimānamūkānāṃ sādhūnāṃ nāsti jīvanam ||[71]
When money disappears, base men survive through begging and petty cheating; good men, made mute by pride of family, do not.

Several verses reveal a sardonic humour in the face of adversity:

dāridrya bhostvam paramaṃ viveki
  guṇādhike puṃsi sadānuraktam |
vidyāvihīne guṇavarjite ca
  muhūrtamātraṃ na ratiṃ karoṣi ||[72]
O Poverty, you are most discriminating! You are ever devoted

to a man of superior virtue, but have not a moment's affection for a worthless ignoramus!

dāridrya śocāmi bhavantamevamasmaccharīre suhṛdityuṣitvā |
vipannadehe mayi mandabhāgye
mameti cintā kva gamiṣyasi tvam ||[73]

O Poverty, I grieve for thee thus: having dwelled in my body, where will you go when my luckless body corrupts?—Such is my worry.

In a much more sombre verse, a poor man bids his life breath to depart:

arthā na santi na ca muñcati māṃ durāśā
dānānna saṅkucati durlalitaṃ mano me |
yācñā ca lāghavakarī svavadhe ca pāpaṃ
prāṇāḥ svayaṃ vrajata kiṃ hi vilambanena ||[74]

There is no money; futile hope will not let me go; and my wanton mind does not shrink from [accepting] charity. Begging belittles one and suicide is a sin—O Breath of Life, depart on your own accord! What good is this procrastination?

Other verses declare that poverty is worse than death. Our last verse implies that indeed poverty is the worst thing in life *or* death:

duḥkhaṃ duḥkhamiti brūyānmānavo narakaṃ prati |
dāridryādadhikaṃ duḥkhaṃ na bhūtaṃ na bhaviṣyati ||[75]

A man may say 'Sorrow! Sorrow!' all the way to hell: there never was nor will be a sorrow greater than poverty.

The few *subhāṣitas* presented above should suffice to indicate what a rich literature of social conscience is contained in the voluminous *saṅgrahas*. These anthologies also present a valuable insight into the milieu of the Sanskrit poets. That contribution will be briefly summarized in the pages which follow.

References

1. Verses of this last type even transcend the requirement of being well-turned: imparting the most prosaic knowledge in crude language. Take, for example, the following verse, which found its way into a celebrated collection known as the *Śārṅgadhara-paddhati* (2255):

To the ingredients consisting of flesh, fat, etc., of fish, hogs and other animals, one should add hot water to the extent required; this should be kept by the wise in a vessel for a fortnight in a lukewarm place; then it becomes the manure *kuṇapa* which richly nourishes the plants.

Trans., Ludwik Sternbach, *Subhāṣita, Gnomic and Didactic Literature*, hereafter abbreviated *SDGL*, vol. IV, Part I of *A History of Indian Literature*, ed., Jan Gonda (Wiesbaden: Otto Harrassowitz, 1974), p. 5.

2. Sternbach, *SGDL*, p. 10.

3. Ed. D.D. Kosambi and V.V. Gokhale as vol. 42 of *HOS*, ed. Daniel H.H. Ingalls (Cambridge, Mass.: 1957); trans. D.H. H. Ingalls as *HOS* 44.

4. Ed. S.C. Banerji (Calcutta: Firma K.L. Mukhopadhyaya, 1965). Hereafter abbreviated as *Skm*.

5. Ed. Embar Krishnamacharya (Baroda: the Oriental Institute, 1938). Hereafter abbreviated *JS*.

6. Ed. Peter Peterson as vol. 37 of the *BSS* (Bombay: 1888). Hereafter abbreviated as *ŚP*.

7. Ed. K. Krishnamoorthy (Dharwar: Karnatak University, 1968). Hereafter abbreviated as *SSSN*.

8. This anthology is the *Subhāṣita-ratna-bhāṇḍāgāra* [hereafter abbreviated as *SRB*], ed. Narayan Ram Acharya (8th edn.; Bombay: Nirnaya Sagar Press, 1952).

9. Cf. Sternbach's 'Subhāṣita-saṃgrahas: A Forgotten Chapter in the Histories of Sanskrit Literature', in *Indologica Taurinensia* (Torino: 1973), vol. I, pp. 169-255.

10. Introduction to the *Mahā-Subhāṣita-Saṃgraha*, (vol. I published simultaneously in Hoshiarpur by the Vishveshvaranand Vedic Research Institute and in Delhi by Motilal Banarsidass, 1974), vol. I, p. lxxiii.

11. *SRB*, '*gṛhasthāśramadūṣaṇam*': 3, p. 89.

12. *SP* 753, *SRB*, '*paragṛhavāsaḥ*': 1, p. 96.

13. *SRB*, '*kṛtaghnanindā*': 1, p. 75; the ed. traces the verse to the *Pañcatantra* (4.11).

14. *SSSN*, '*Tapaḥpaddhati*': 1, p. 29.

15. Loc. cit., 2.

16. Peter Peterson, ed., *The Subhāṣitāvalī of Vallabhadeva*, [hereafter abbreviated *VS*], no. 31 of the Bombay Sanskrit and Prakrit Series (reprinted, Poona: Bhandarkar Institute Press, 1961), no. 2323, p. 400.

17. Ibid., no. 164, p. 26; *SRB*, '*kupaṇḍitanindā*': 75, p. 41. *VS* ascribes the poem to one Bhāgavata-viṅka.

18. *VS* 2319; *SRB* '*kuvaidyanindā*': 2, p 44.

19. *SRB*, '*kuvaidyanindā*': 1, p. 44.

20. Loc. cit., 7.

21. Loc. cit., '*kugaṇakanindā*': 2. Both were only created to steal money; both display their *pañcāṅgas*, which means either 'five parts of the body', or 'an ephemeris'.

22. Loc. cit., 3.

23. Loc. cit., 4.

24. Loc. cit., 5.

25. Ibid., *'kāyasthanindā'*: 1, p. 45; *VS* 2324, p. 400.
26. *SP* 4045; *SRB* loc cit., 3. In his *Narmamālā*, Kṣemendra gives his own version of the origin of the term *divira*. The patriarch of the Kāyasthas has just lamented the defeat of the demons at the hands of the gods. Kali appears to console him with a new weapon (the pen) and says the following:

daityakṣaye kṛte yasmādbhavatā divi roditam !
tasmāttvaṃ diviro nāma bhuvi khyāto bhaviṣyati // (1.15)

27. *SP* 4043; *VS* 2326; *SRB* loc. cit., 2.
28. *VS* 2363.
29. *SRB*, *'kupaṇḍitanindā'*: 8.
30. Loc. cit., 11.
31. Loc. cit., 1.
32. Ibid., *'chāndasanindā'*: 1, p. 42.
33. Ibid., *'mīmāṃsakanindā'*: 1, p. 43.
34. Loc. cit., 2.
35. The commentary adds that Brāhmaṇa is *'pratītapadārthaiḥ sahāvicālyaḥ'* or 'incapable of being displaced by facile categorization'.
36. Loc. cit., *'naiyāyikanindā'*: 7.
37. Loc. cit., 9.
38. Loc. cit., 10.
39. Ibid., *'vaiyākaraṇanindā'*: 2, p. 42.
40. Ibid., *'kupaṇḍitanindā'*: 66, p. 41.
41. *E.g.*, ibid., 12, p. 39.
42. Ibid., 34, p. 40.
43. Loc. cit., 36.
44. Ibid., 9, p. 39.
45. Loc. cit., 10.
46. *E.g.*, ibid., *'svabhāvavarṇanam'*: 5, p. 84.
47. Loc. cit., 10 (attributed to *Mbh.* 5.1134).
48. *VS* 2400, p. 412.
49. II.9 Cf. above, the close of chapter 3.
50. The text in *VS* reads *'khagṛhiṇī'*; surely a misprint.
51. *SSSN* 1.26.7; p. 33.
52. *SRB*, *'kupaṇḍitanindā'*: 72, p 41.
53. Ibid., *'dhananindā'*: 2, p. 64. *'Lakṣmivantaḥ'*, of course, is a pun relating to Viṣṇu as well.
54. Loc. cit., 4; *SP* 341.
55. The commentary declares that because Ḍa-kāra and La-kāra are of the same *varṇa* *'jala'* may be read for *'jaḍa'*. This assertion of the homogeneity of the two letters, incidentally, is contrary to Bhaṭṭoji Dīkṣita's *vṛtti* on Pāṇini 1.1.9, where La-kāra is said to be dental. Cf., the *Siddhānta-Kaumudī* with the *Bālamanoramā*, ed. Gopal Sastri Nene, (Varanasi: Chowkhamba Sanskrit Series, 1969), vol. I, p. 12.
56. Loc. cit., 5; *SP* 342.
57. Loc. cit., 6.
58. Ibid., *'kupaṇḍitanindā'*: 73, p. 41.
59. *VS* 2335, p. 401. The verse is attributed to Prakāśavarsa.

60. Loc. cit., 2337. The verse is attributed to Icchaṭa.
61. *SRB 'kupaṇḍitanindā'*: 55, p. 40; *Pañcatantra* 1.255.
62. Ibid., *'sevakanindā'*: 16, p. 97; *Hitopadeśa* 1.158.
63. Loc. cit., 17; *Pañcatantra* 1.306.
64. Loc. cit., 7; *VS* 3214 (p. 530) offers a variant reading and ascribes the verse to Vyāsa.
65. Ibid., *'daridranindā'*: 12, p. 66.
66. Loc. cit., 24; *VS* 3167 (p. 523), where the verse is attributed to Vyāsa.
67. Loc. cit., 2 (p. 65); *ŚP* 402.
68. Loc. cit., 3; variants are found in *VS* 3160 and Mbh. 12.321.88.
69. Loc. cit., 28 (p. 66); *VS* 3172, p. 524.
70. Loc. cit., 27; *VS* 3171.
71. Loc. cit., 31.
72. Loc. cit., 41.
73. Loc. cit., 42.
74. Loc. cit., 50, p. 67.
75. Loc. cit., 13; *Prasaṅgābharaṇam* 17.

Chapter 6

THE ACHIEVEMENT OF SANSKRIT LITERATURE: A REASSESSMENT

The Cultural Matrices of Sanskrit Poetry

The *subhāṣita* collections provide valuable insights into the environment within which the Sanskrit poets worked. There we quickly learn that poets often condemned bad poets, plagiarism and the ornate mannerism which has so bothered modern critics. But, ornamentation is also defended, while captious critics are damned. Last, and most important, the poets themselves condemn the prostitution of their art in the context of royal patronage.

On the Faults of Poets

Is there anything worse than a bad poet? That is the theme of the following verses:

> *nākavitvamadharmāya mṛtaye daṇḍanāya ca |*
> *kukavitvaṃ punaḥ sākṣānmṛtimāhurmanīṣiṇaḥ ||*[1]
> There is no sin, punishment of death in not being a poet; but the wise declare that being a *bad* poet is Death incarnate.
> *kukaveḥ kavicorastu varaṃ yaḥ sujanān svayā |*
> *nodvejayedduruktyā ca sūktya cāsya praharṣayet ||*[2]
> But it is better to be a plagiarist than a bad poet: better to amuse with good verse rather than abuse with one's own doggerel!

Another verse compares poets to slobbering infants, unable to set their feet (pun intended) down properly and boring men with their prattle.[3] Still another berates the empty pedantry of logicians, but finds them superior to poets, who compose hymns of praise to the form of a prostitute's breast.[4]

Several verses condemn plagiarism. The following is one example:

anyavarṇaparāvṛttyā bandhacihnanigūhanaiḥ |
anākhyātaḥ satāṃ madhye kaviścauro vibhāvyate ||[5]
By changing the letters of another's [composition] and concealing the connection, a plagiarist is fancied a poet among trusting souls.

The next verse, however, declares that an imitative hack can never approach the achievement of a great poet:

paraślokānstokānanudivasamabhyasya nanu ye catuṣpādīṃ kuryurbahava iha te santi kavayaḥ |
avicchinnodgacchajjaladhilaharīrītisuhṛdaḥ suhṛdyā vaiśadyaṃ dadhati kila keṣāṃcana giraḥ ||[6]
Surely there are many poets in this world who, after imitating daily the minor verses of others, are able to compose a stanza. [Yet,] it seems that the words of only a few are so pleasing as to convey the beauty of a succession of waves rising unbroken from the sea.

On Poetic Ornamentation

As long ago as the twelfth century, the Kashmiri poet Maṅkhaka voiced regret that Sanskrit poetry had degenerated to a condition of clever, but manneristic artificiality:

yātāste rasasārasaṅgrahavidhiṃ niṣpīḍya niṣpīḍya ye vāktattvekṣulatāṃ purā katipaye tattvaspṛśaścakrire |
jāyante'dya yathāyathaṃ tu kavayaste tatra saṃtanvate ye 'nuprāsakaṭhoracitrayamakaśleṣādiśalkoccayam ||[7]
Gone are those few poets who touched truth after repeatedly pressing the sugar cane of poetic speech and extracting its essence (*rasa*). Today, the poets born in their place only squeeze the dried pulp of alliteration, difficult words, elaborate word-play (*citras*),[8] puns and so forth.

But poetic ornamentation did have its defenders. One of them was another Kashmiri, Baka, who lived in the fifteenth century. He declares that such ornamentation is indispensable to good poetry:

yaḥ syātkevalalakṣyalakṣaṇarato no tarkasaṃparkabhṛn nālaṅkāravicāracārudhiṣaṇaḥ kāvyajñaśikṣojjhitaḥ |

tasmāccedrasaśāli kāvyamudayedekāntataḥ sundaraṃ prāsādo dhavalastadā kṣitipate kākasya kārṣṇyādbhavet //[9]

Could a lovely *kāvya*, rich in sentiment, come from one solely interested in the plain delineation of his subject, one with no familiarity with logic, one whose mind has not been graced by a study of poetic ornaments, one unschooled by literary authorities? If that could happen, O King, then a dazzling white palace could arise from the blackness of a crow!

Indeed, the conflicting standards of aesthetic excellence re-reflected in the two verses quoted just above must have placed poets in a bind. Maṅkhaka, again, expresses beautifully the frustration inherent in such a situation:

artho'sti cenna padaśuddhirathāsti sāpi no rītirasti yadi sā ghaṭanā kutastyā /
sāpyasti cenna navavakragatistadetad vyarthaṃ vinā rasamaho gahanaṃ kavitvam //[10]

If there is meaning, then there is no 'refinement of diction'. If there is that, then there is no 'stylistic excellence'. If there is that, then 'where is its unity?' If there is that, then there is no 'novelty'; then, 'this is *meaningless* without sentiment!' Alas, it is impossible to be a poet!

On Critics

Judging from the rather large number of verses directed against them, critics must have posed a formidable threat to Sanskrit poets. One poet compared critics who fault excellent verse with the villains who brought the chaste Sītā to the purifying fire.[11] Another says that those who find fault with charming verse may be likened to a swarm of insects which only seeks out a wound in a lovely body.[12] Still another says that while the graceful *haṃsas* frolic on a lotus-covered lake, a *krauñca* bird doubles over and roots for snails.[13] Similarly, it is said that a camel intruding on a pleasure garden regards it as only a thicket of thorns.[14]

While the critics continue to be compared to one odious or clumsy thing after another, some of the comparisons seem to border on playful humour more than on bitterness. One poet states that the fault-finding critics project their own failings onto the verse they criticize, like a small-breasted woman blaming her *kañcuka* garment.[15] Another poet with a similar bent of mind composed the following:

> *ślokārthasvādakāle tu śabdotpattivicintakāḥ |*
> *nīvīvimokṣavelāyāṃ vastramaulyavicintakāḥ ||*[16]
>
> Those who stop to worry over the grammatical authority of a word at the moment of savouring the meaning of a verse [are like] those who, when pulling off a woman's under-garment, stop to worry about its price.

A good many verses depict captious critics as simply envious of poetic genius.[17] Yet, in spite of an often hostile critical environment, Sanskrit poets might take heart in Jagannātha Paṇḍitarāja's verse which consoled his poetic voice not to despair on account of the malicious attacks of the envious, but rather to consider that it will bring pleasure to the true connoisseurs of verse.[18]

Against Patronage

Long before modern critics, Sanskrit poets blamed patronage for its stifling influence on poetic creation. One poet put it that when even Viṣṇu retires to escape the flattery, his wife, Lakṣmī's[19] career is sung in epic terms. So might a king, the poet says, bedeck with pearls the body of a bitch.[20] Another complains that poets take captivating poetic speech and devote it entirely to niggardly and treacherous kings.[21] Kṣemendra says it this way:

> *kavibhirnṛpasevāsu citrālaṅkārahāriṇī |*
> *vāṇī veśyeva lobhena paropakaraṇikṛtā ||*[22]
>
> In the service of kings, poets have greedily prostituted poetic speech—captivating in its lovely ornaments—[23] like a common whore.

Kṣemendra was obviously no 'talking house bird'.

Recapitulation

It may well be, as A. B. Keith puts it, that the *Abhijñāna-śākuntala* moves 'in a narrow world far removed from the cruelty of real life', but the same judgement cannot be applied to the verses on poverty collected in the *subhāṣita* anthologies. It is also true that, as S. K. De has it, the work of the Sanskrit poet 'is very often nothing more than a delicate blossom of fancy, fostered in a world of tranquil calm', but that world is markedly in contrast to the world of Kṣemendra's satires, the *bhāṇas* and *prahasanas*. And if priests and kings play a dominant role in Sanskrit literature (as they did in the society it reflects), we have seen abundant criticism of both in every preceding chapter. It seems reasonable to conclude then that a significant literature of social conscience *does* exist in Sanskrit and that Keith's pronouncement that 'we can trace [there] no echo of social discontent' cannot hold true for all the classics, much less for the vast literature which lies beyond the standard curricula in Sanskrit education. There exists today both an opportunity and a need for detailed studies of the dimensions of social conscience in the satires, *bhāṇas*, *prahasanas* and *subhāṣitas*. It has been the aim of this essay to lay the groundwork for such detailed studies.

References

1. *SSSN* 2.51.1, p. 101, where it is attributed to Bhāmaha.
2. Loc. cit., 2.
3. *SRB 'kukavinindā'*: 1, p. 37; *ŚP* 191. Cf. *SSRB* loc. cit., 10, where poets are compared to whoremasters.
4. *SRB 'naiyāyikanindā'*: 4, p. 43.
5. *SRB 'kukavinindā'*: 3, p. 37; *ŚP* 196.
6. *SRB* 'kupaṇḍitanindā': 60, p. 41. The verse is attributed to Maṅkhaka.
7. *SRB*, loc. cit., 76, pp. 41–2; *VS* 178, p. 29. Cf. *SRB*, loc. cit., 52, p. 40.
8. For citras, cf. Gerow, op. cit., pp. 175ff.
9. *SRB 'kukavinindā'*: 30, p. 38; *VS* 192, p. 32.
10. *SRB 'kupaṇḍitanindā'*: 53, p. 40; *VS* 176, pp. 28–9.
11. *SSSN* 2.51.3, p. 101.
12. *SRB 'kukavinindā'*: 14, p. 38.
13. Ibid., *'kupaṇḍitanindā'*: 70, p. 41. The source is given as the *Padyasaṅgraha* of Kavibhaṭṭa.
14. Ibid., *'kukavinindā'*: 17, p. 38; *SP* 144.
15. Loc. cit., 13; the *Bhojaprabandha* of Ballāḷa 97.
16. Loc. cit., 8.
17. E.g., loc. cit., 63-65, p. 41; *SP* 205-7. *SRB* loc. cit., 71.
18. Loc. cit., 50, p. 40; *Bhāminīvilāsa* 4.40.
19. The term also means 'wealth'.

20. Loc. cit., 25, p. 38.
21. Loc. cit., 26.
22. *Darpadalana* 3.10, p. 165, of the Hyderabad edition. The same verse with the variant reading, *vittālaṅkārakāriṇī* occurs anonymously in *SRB*, loc. cit., 2, p. 37 and *ŚP* 155.
23. For the other meaning of *citta*, cf. above, n. 8.

BIBLIOGRAPHY

Abrams, M.H. *A Glossary of Literary Terms.* New York: Holt, Rinehart and Winston, 1961.

Acharya, Narayan Ram, ed., the *Subhāṣita-Ratna-Bhāṇḍāgāra.* 8th edn., rev. and enl. Bombay: Nirnaya Sagar Press, 1952.

Amitagati, *Subhāṣitasamdoha,* parts X-XVI printed with a German translation by Richard Schmidt and Johannes Hertel, *Zeitschrift der Deutschen Morgenländischen Gesellschaft,* vol. 59, 1905, pp. 523-77; parts XXIV XXIX printed with a German Translation by Richard Schmidt, *ZDMG,* vol. 61, 1907, pp. 298-341.

An Anthology of Sanskrit Court Poetry: Vidyākara's 'Subhāṣita Ratnakośa', Daniel H.H. Ingalls, trans. vol. 44 of the *Harvard Oriental Series,* ed. Daniel H.H. Ingalls. Cambridge, Mass.: Harvard University Press, 1965.

Apte, V.S. *The Practical Sanskrit-English Dictionary,* Gode, P.K., and C.G. Karve, et al., eds. 3 vols. Poona: Prasad Prakashan, 1957-59. 6 appendices.

Bamzai, Prithvi Nath Kaul. *A History of Kashmir.* New Delhi: Metropolitan Book Co. Ltd., 2nd rev. edn., 1973.

Bandhu, Visva, ed., *A Grammatical Word-index to the Four Vedas,* in two vols. Hoshiarpur: Vishveshvaranand Vedic Research Institute, 1960 (vol. I) and 1963 (vol. II).

Banerji, Sures Chandra. *A Companion to Sanskrit Literature.* Delhi, 1971.

Basham, A.L. *The Wonder that was India.* New York: Grove Press, Inc., 1959. xxi, 568 pp. Illus., maps, appdcs., index.

The *Bhāgavata-Purāṇa,* Sanskrit text and English translation by C.L. Goswami in 2 vols. Gorakhpur: Gita Press, 1971.

Bhattacharya, Jagadishwara. *Hāsyārṇava-prahasanam,* ed. with the 'Prabhā' Hindi commentary by Ishwar Prasad Chaturvedi, no. 103 of *The Vidyābhawan Sanskrit Granthamālā.* Varanasi: The Chowkhamba Vidyabhawan, 1963.

Bloomfield, Maurice, 'On False Ascetics and Nuns in Hindu Fiction', *Journal of the American Oriental Society,* XLIV (1924), pp. 202-42.

———'The Character and Adventures of Mūladeva', *Proceedings of the American Philosophical Society*, LII (Jan.-April 1913), pp. 616-50.

Bodhayana, the *Bhagavadajjuka* (or, *Bhagavadajjukiya*), ed. Prabhakara Sastri Veturi. Madras: Vavilla Press, 1925.

Budhendra, Ramacandra, *Suhṛdayanandinī*, a Sanskrit commentary published in the *Subhāsitatriśatī*, ed. D.D. Kosambi and N.R. Acarya. Bombay: Nirnaya Sagar Press, 1957.

Burrow, T. *The Sanskrit Language*. London, 1955.

Caturbhāṇī [the running title; the jacket gives 'Srngar-Hat'], ed. with Hindi trans. by Moticandra and V.S. Agrawal. Bombay: Hindi Granth Ratnakar Karyalay Pvt. Ltd., 1959.

Crawford, S. Cromwell. *The Evolution of Hindu Ethical Ideals*. Calcutta: Firma K.L. Mukhopadhyaya, 1974.

Dāmodaragupta's *Kuṭṭanīmatam-Kāvyam*, ed. by Madhusudan Kaul, Work No. 266, Fascicle I (Issue no. 1551, N.S.) of the *Bibliotheca Indica* series. Calcutta: the Royal Asiatic Society of Bengal, 1944.

Danielou, Alain. *Hindu Polytheism*. New York: Pantheon Books, 1964.

Dasgupta, S.N., and S.K. De, *A History of Sanskrit Literature: Classical Period*. Calcutta, 1962.

Dattaray, Rajatbaran. *A Critical Survey of the Life and Works of Kṣemendra*. Calcutta: Sanskrit Pustak Bhandar, 1974.

De, S.K., 'A Note on the Sanskrit Monologue-Play (Bhāṇa), with Special Reference to the Caturbhāṇī', *Journal of the Royal Asiatic Society*, 1926, pp. 63-90.

———'Wit, Humour and Satire in Ancient Indian Literature', *Our Heritage*, vol. III, Part II (July-December 1955), pp. 157-80.

Devadhar, C.R., ed. and trans., *Dramas of Kālidāsa*, vol. I of *Works of Kālidāsa*. Delhi: Motilal Banarsidass, 1966.

Dialogues of the Buddha: Translated from the Pali of the Digha Nikāya by T.W. Rhys Davids and C.A.F. Rhys Davids. vol. II. No. 3 in the *Sacred Books of the Buddhists*, ed. F. Max-Müller. London: Oxford University Press, 1910.

Edgerton, Franklin. *The Panchatantra Reconstructed*. vols. I and II of the *American Oriental Series*. New Haven, Conn.: the American Oriental Society, 1924.

Emeneau, M.B. *A Union List of Printed Indic Texts and Trans-*

lations in American Libraries. vol. VII of the *American Oriental Series*, ed. W. Norman Brown, John K. Shryock, and E.A. Speiser. New Haven, 1935.

Gerow, Edwin. *A Glossary of Indian Figures of Speech*. The Hague: Mouton & Co., 1971.

Gonda, J., 'The So-Called Secular, Humorous and Satirical Hymns of the Ṛgveda', in *Orientalia Neederlandica*, a volume of Oriental studies published under the auspices of the Netherlands' Oriental Society (Oostersch Genootschap in Nederland). Leiden: 1948, pp. 312-48.

Gupta, Dharmendra Kumar. *Society and Culture in the Time of Daṇḍin*. Delhi: Meharchand Lachhmandas, 1972.

Hertel, Johannes, ed., *The Panchatantra... in the Recension, called Panchākhyānaka*... vol. 11 of the *Harvard Oriental Series*, ed., Charles Rockwell Lanman. Cambridge, Mass.: Harvard University Press, 1908.

———ed., *The Panchatantra... in its oldest recension, the Kashmirian, entitled Tantrākhyayikā*, vol. 14 of the *Harvard Oriental Series*, ed., Charles Rockwell Lanman. Cambridge, Mass.: Harvard University Press, 1915.

———ed., *The Thirty-two Bharataka Stories*, no. 2 of the series of the *Forschungsinstitut Für Indogermanistik Indische Abteilung, Sächsische Forshungsinstitute in Leipzig*. Leipzig: 1921.

Highet, Gilbert. *The Anatomy of Satire*. Princeton, N.J.: Princeton University Press, 1962.

Ingalls, Daniel H.H., 'Kālidāsa and the Attitudes of the Golden Age', *Journal of the American Oriental Society*, 96, no. 1 (Jan.-March 1976), pp. 15-26.

Jagannātha Paṇḍitarāja's *Bhāminīvilāsa* with the commentary of Jivananda Vidyasagara, ed. Ashubodha Vidyabhusana and Nityabodha Vidyaratna. Calcutta: Vacaspatya Press, 1936.

Jalhaṇa's *Sūktimuktāvali*, ed. with an introduction in Sanskrit by Embar Krishnamacharya. Baroda: The Oriental Institute, 1938.

Jhalakikar, Vamanacarya, ed. and author of a Sanskrit commentary on the *Kāvyaprakāśa of Mammaṭa*, 7th edn. Poona: Bhandarkar Oriental Research Institute, 1965.

Johnston, E.H., ed. and trans., *The Buddhacarita or Acts of the Buddha*. Lahore, 1936. Reprinted Delhi, 1972.

Jong, J.W. de, Review of *A Reader on the Sanskrit Grammarians*,

J.F. Staal, ed., *The Indo-Iranian Journal*, XVI, no. 3 (1975), pp. 227-29.

Kale, M.R., ed. and trans., *Bāṇa's Kādambarī*. 4th rev. edn., Delhi: Motilal Banarsidass, 1968.

———ed. and trans., *The Daśakumāracarita of Daṇḍin*. 4th edn. Delhi: Motilal Banarsidass, 1966.

———ed. and trans., *The Nīti and Vairāgya Śatakas of Bhartṛhari*. 7th edn. Delhi: Motilal Banarsidass, 1971.

Kalhaṇa's *Rājataraṅgiṇī*, 'A Chronical of the Kings of Kasmir', trans. M.A. Stein, 2 vols. Delhi: Motilal Banarsidass, 1961.

Kalhaṇa's *Rājataraṅgiṇī*, edited by Vishva Bandhu in collaboration with Bhima Dev, K.S. Ramaswami Sastri and S. Bhas karan Nair as vols. 5 and 6 of the *Woolner Indological Series*. Hoshiarpur: Vishveshvaranand Vedic Research Institute, 1963: Part I (Taraṅgas I-VIII); 1965: Part II (Taraṅga VIII).

Kālidāsa's *Abhijñāna-Śākuntala* with the commentary *Arthadyotanikā* of Rāghava Bhaṭṭa. 12th edn., re-edited by Narayan Ram Acharya. Bombay: Nirnaya Sagar Press, 1958.

Kālidāsa's *Raghuvaṃśa* with the commentary *Sañjīvinī* of Mallinātha and extracts from several other commentaries. 11th edn., edited by Narayan Ram Acharya. Bombay: Nirnaya Sagar Press, 1948.

Keith, A. Berriedale. *A History of Sanskrit Literature*. London, 1920.

———, *The Religion and Philosophy of the Vedas and Upanishads*. vol. XXXII of the *Harvard Oriental Series*, ed. C.R. Lanman. Cambridge, Mass.: Harvard University Press, 1925.

———, *The Sanskrit Drama in its Origin, Development, Theory and Practice*. London: Oxford University Press, 1924.

Kosambi, D.D. *Myth and Reality: Studies in the Formation of Indian Culture*. Bombay: Popular Prakashan, 1962.

Kosambi, D.D. and Narayan Ram Acarya, eds., *Subhāṣitatriśatī* (the three *śatakas* of Bhartṛhari). Bombay: Nirnaya Sagara Press, 1957.

Kosambi, D.D. and V.V. Gokhale, eds., *The Subhāṣitaratnakośa compiled by Vidyākara*, vol. 42 of the *Harvard Oriental Series*, ed. Daniel H.H. Ingalls. Cambridge, Mass.: Harvard University Press, 1957.

Kṛṣṇa-miśra's *Prabodha-candrodaya*, ed. with the 'Prakāśa' Sanskrit-Hindi commentaries by Ramacandra Misra. vol. 14 in

The Vidyābhawan Sanskrit Granthamālā. Varanasi: The Chowkhamba Vidyabhawan, 1968.

Kṣemendra's *Deśopadeśa* and *Narmamālā*, ed. with Preface and Introduction by Madhusudana Kaul. No. 40 in the *Kashmir Series of Texts and Studies.* Poona: The Aryabhushan Press, 1923.

Kṣemendra's *Kalāvilāsa* in *Kāvyamālā.* Part I, ed. Durgaprasad and K.P. Parab. Bombay: Nirnaya Sagara Press, 1886.

Kṣemendra's *Kalāvilāsa*: V-X, trans. into German by Richard Schmidt in *Wiener Zeitschrift für die Kunde des Morgenlandes*, XXVIII (1941), pp. 406-35.

Levi, Silvain, 'La Bṛhatkathāmañjarī de Kṣemendra', *Journal Asiatique*, Ser. VIII, Tome VI (Nov./Dec., 1885), pp. 397-479.

Lorenzen, David N. *The Kāpālikas and Kālamukhas: Two Lost Śaivite Sects*, vol. XII of the *Australian National University Centre of Oriental Studies, Oriental Monograph Series.* New Delhi: Thomson Press (India) Limited, 1972.

Lüders, H. *Bruchstücke der Kalpanāmaṇḍitikā des Kumāralāta* in *Kongel Preuss Turfan-Expeditionen*, Kleinere Sanskrit-Texte II. Leipzig, 1926.

The *Mahābhārata*, with Nīlakaṇṭha's Commentary, no editor listed in the 1st vol. In the last 6 vols., the edn. is listed as Ramacandrasastri Kinjawadekar. 7 vols. (including the *Harivaṃśa*). Poona: Citrasala Press, 1929-35.

Mahalingam, T.V. *Kancipuram in Early South Indian History.* Bombay, 1968.

Mahendravikramavarman's *Mattavilāsa-prahasanam*, with the 'Prakāśa' Hindi commentary of Kapiladeva Giri, vol. 135 of *The Vidyābhawan Sanskrit Granthamālā.* Varanasi: Chowkhamba Vidyabhawan, 1966.

———, trans. as *Die Streiche des Berauschten* by Johannes Hertel. Leipzig: H. Haessel, 1924.

Majumdar, R.C. et al. *Advanced History of India.* 2nd edn. London: 1950.

The *Manusmṛti* with the commentary, *Manvarthamuktāvali*, of Kullūkabhaṭṭa, ed. by Narayanatmaja Viththala Sarma. Bombay: Nirnaya Sagara Press, 1887.

The *Manusmṛti* with the commentary of Medhātithi, ed. by

Manasukharay Mor in two volumes. Calcutta: Udayacala Press, 1967, 71.

'Matta-vilāsa: a Farce by Mahendravikramavarman', Barnett, L.D., trans., *Bulletin of the School of Oriental Studies*, vol. 5 (1928-30), pp. 697-717.

Miller, Barbara Stoler, ed. and trans., *Bhartṛhari: Poems*. New York: Columbia University Press, 1967.

Minoru, Hara, Review of *The Kāpālikas and Kālamukhas: Two Lost Śaivite Sects*, by David N. Lorenzen, *The Indo-Iranian Journal*, VIII, Nos. 3/4 (Nov./Dec. 1975), p. 259.

Monier-Williams, Monier, *A Sanskrit-English Dictionary*. New edn., rev. and enl. by the author, E. Leumann, C. Cappeller, et al., Reprinted, Delhi: Motilal Banarsidass, 1970.

Mudholkar, Srinivasa Katti, ed., *The Vālmīki-Rāmāyaṇa* with three Sanskrit commentaries in 7 vols. Bombay: no date given on early volumes. Last volume dated 1920.

Muir, J., *Original Sanskrit Texts on the Origin and History of the People of India*. 5 vols. London, 1870.

Mukhopadhyaya, Sujitkumar. *The Vajrasūcī of Aśvaghoṣa: a, Study of the Sanskrit Text and Chinese Version*. Santiniketan 1960.

Müller, F. Max. *A History of Ancient Sanskrit Literature so far as it illustrates the Primitive Religion of the Brahmans*. Reprinted, Varanasi, 1968.

Nalla-Diksita's *Śṛṅgāra-sarvasva-bhāṇa*, ed. Sivadatta and V. I. S. Pansikar, vol. 78 of *The Kāvyamālā Series*. Bombay: Nirnaya Sagara Press, 1925.

Nandargikar, Gopal Raghunath, ed. and trans., *The Raghuvaṃśa of Kālidāsa with the Commentary of Mallinātha*. 4th edn. Delhi: Motilal Banarsidass, 1971.

Nene, Gopal Shastri, ed., *The Siddhānta Kaumudī of Bhaṭṭoji Dīkṣita* with the *Bālamanoramā* commentary of Vāsudeva Dīkṣita. no. 136 of the *Kashi Sanskrit Series*. 4 vols. Varanasi: The Chowkhamba Sanskrit Series Office, 1969.

The Ocean of Story, a translation of Somadeva's *Kathāsaritsāgara* by C. H. Tawney, ed., N. M. Penzer. 10 vols. Reprinted Delhi: Motilal Banarsidass, 1968.

The *Padyasaṅgraha* of Kavibhaṭṭa in the *Kāvya-saṅgraha*, ed. J. Haeberlin. Calcutta: W. Thacker and Co., 1847.

Pansikar, Laxman Shastri, ed., *The Yājñavalkyasmṛti* with the *Mitāksarā* commentary of Vijñāneśvara. 2nd edn. Bombay: Nirnaya Sagara Press, 1918.

Parab, Kasinath, ed., *The Bhojaprabandha of Ballāla*. 2nd edn. Bombay: Nirnaya Sagara Press, 1904.

Patañjali's *Mahābhāṣya*, in 3 vols. (with Kaiyaṭa's *Pradīpa* and Nāgeśabhaṭṭa's *Udyota*). Delhi: Motilal Banarsidass, 1967.

Peterson, Peter, ed., *The Paddhati of Śārṅgadhara, a Sanskrit Anthology* vol. I; vol. 37 of *The Bombay Sanskrit Series*. Bombay: Government Central Book Depot, 1888.

Peterson, Peter and Durgaprasad, eds., *The Subhāṣitāvali of Vallabhadeva*. 2nd edn., by Raghunath Damodar Karmarkar, no. XXXI of *The Bombay Sanskrit and Prakrit Series*. Poona: Bhandarkar Institute Press, 1961.

Potter, Karl H. *The Encyclopedia of Indian Philosophies*, vol. I: Bibliography. Delhi, 1970.

The *Prasaṅgābharaṇa* of Kulatilaka. Bombay: Gopal Narayan and Co., (no date).

Raghavacharya, E. V. V. and D. G. Padhye, eds., *Kṣemendra-laghukāvya-saṅgraha*: '*Minor Works of Kṣemendra*', no. 7 of the *Sanskrit Academy Series*, ed. Aryendra Sharma. Hyderabad: the Sanskrit Academy, Osmania University, 1961.

Raghavan, V., 'Presidential Address' in *Proceedings and Transactions of the* 21*st All India Oriental Conference* (1961). vol. I. pp. 1-57.

Ṛgveda Brāhmaṇas: *The Aitareya and Kauśītaki Brāhmaṇas of the Rig-veda*, trans. A. B. Keith. vol. XXV of the *Harvard Oriental Series*, ed. C. R. Lanman. Cambridge, Mass.: Harvard University Press, 1920.

Sachau, Karl Eduard, ed. and trans., *Al-Biruni's India*. London: K. Paul, Trench, Trübner and Co., Ltd., 1910.

The Sacred Laws of the Aryas, as Taught in the Schools of Āpastamba, Gautama, Vasishṭha and Baudhāyana. Part II, trans. by George Bühler. vol. 14 in *The Sacred Books of The East*, ed. F. Max Müller. Oxford: the Clarendon Press, 1882.

Sankalia, H. D., 'Dohad Inscriptions of Mahmood Begra', in *Epigraphia Indica*.

Śaṅkaramiśra's *Gaurīdigambara-prahasanam*, ed. with the 'Prakāśa' Hindi commentary by Tarinisa Jha, vol. 283 of

The Haridas Sanskrit Series. Varanasi: The Chowkhamba Sanskrit Series Office, 1969.

Śaṅkhadhara's *Laṭakamelakam-prahasanam*, with the 'Prakāśa' Hindi commentary by Kapiladeva Giri, vol. 87 of *The Vidyābhawan Sanskrit Granthamālā*. Varanasi: Chowkhamba Vidyabhawan, 1962.

Sankrtyayan, Rahul. *The Dhammapadam: Pali Text with Sanskrit Chaya and Hindi Translation*. Lucknow, 1965.

Sastri, Haraprasad, 'The Discovery of a Work by Āryadeva in Sanskrit', *Journal of the Asiatic Society of Bengal*, LXVII (1898), pp. 175-84.

Sastri, Haraprasad, 'The Northern Buddhism, [Part] III', *The Indian Historical Quarterly*, I (1925), pp. 464-72.

Sastri, Haraprasad. *Saundarananda Kāvya of Ārya Bhadanta Aśvaghoṣa*. Pub. in the *Bibliotheca Indica Series* by the Royal Asiatic Society of Bengal. Calcutta, 1939.

Sastri, Jagadis Lal, ed., *The Kathāsaritsāgara*. Delhi: Motilal Banarsidass, 1970.

Sāyaṇa's *Subhāṣita-Sudhānidhi*, critically edited with an Introduction by K. Krishnamoorthy. Dharwar: Karnatak University, 1968.

Schokker, G. H., ed., *The Pādatāḍitaka of Śyāmilaka*, Part I: A Text Critical Edition by G. H. Schokker; Part II: A Translation and Word-Index by G. H. Schokker and P. J. Worsley. Part I: The Hague: Mouton & Co., 1966. Part II: Dordrecht, Holland: D. Reidel Publ. Co., 1976.

Sharma, Aryendra, ed., *Paṇḍitarāja-Kāvya-Saṅgraha*. No. 2 of the *Sanskrit Academy Series*, ed. Aryendra Sharma. Hyderabad: The Sanskrit Academy, Osmania University, 1958.

Sharma, Batuk Nath, and Baladeva Upadhyaya, eds., the *Nāṭyaśāstra* of Bharata, no. 60 in the Kashi Sanskrit Series. Varanasi: Chowkhamba Sanskrit Series Office, 1929.

Shastri, Ajaya Mitra. *India as Seen in the Kuttanī-Mata of Dāmodaragupta*. Delhi: Motilal Banarsidass, 1975.

Sorensen, S. *An Index to the Names in the Mahābhārata*. Reprinted Delhi: Motilal Banarsidass, 1963.

Staal, J. F., ed., *A Reader on the Sanskrit Grammarians*. Cambridge, Mass.: the MIT Press, 1972.

Sternbach, Ludwik, comp., *Gaṇikā-vṛtta-saṅgraha*. No. 4 of the

Vishveshvaranand Indological Series. Hoshiarpur: Vishveshvaranand Vedic Research Institute, 1953.

———, comp., *Mahā-subhāṣita-saṅgraha*. Vol. I, no. 64 of the *Vishveshvaranand Indological Series*. Hoshiarpur: Vishveshvaranand Vedic Research Institute, 1974.

———, *Subhāṣita, Gnomic and Didactic Literature*, a contribution to vol. IV, Part I of *A History of Indian Literature*, ed. Jan Gonda. Wiesbaden: Otto Harrassowitz, 1974.

Suryakanta, *Kṣemendra Studies*, no. 91 in the *Poona Oriental Series*, ed. H. L. Hariyappa. Poona: Oriental Book Agency, 1954.

Tagore, Rabindranath, 'Kalantara', in *Rabindra Racanāvali*, vol. 13, pp. 209-16.

Tarkavachaspati, Taranatha, *Vācaspatyam*, in 6 vols. Varanasi: Chowkhamba Sanskrit Series, 1961-62 (reprinted edition).

The Ten Princes, Arthur W. Ryder, trans. Chicago: The University of Chicago Press, 1927.

Thomas, F. W., 'Four Sanskrit Plays', *Centenary Supplement to the Journal of the Royal Asiatic Society of Great Britain and Ireland*, Oct., 1924, pp. 123-36.

Van Buitenen, J. A. B. *Two Plays of Ancient India*. New York: Columbia University Press, 1968.

Vatsarāja, Amatya. *Hāsya-cūḍāmaṇi-prahasanam*, ed. Jaya Shankar Tripathy, Prayaga: Devbhasa Prakasan, 1970-71.

Venkatacharya, T. and A. K. Warder, eds. and trans., *The Ubhayābhisārikā or 'Both Go To Meet' by Vararuci*. Madras: V. Sambamurthy, 1967.

The *Viṣṇu-Purāṇa*, Sanskrit text and Hindi trans. by Muni Lal Gupta. Gorakhpur: Gita Press, 1969.

Winternitz, M. *A History of Indian Literature*. Vol. I, Pt. I trans. from the original German by S. Ketar. 3rd edn., University of Calcutta, 1962. Vol. II trans. by S. Ketar and H. Kohn revised by the author and published University of Calcutta, 1933. Vol. III, Fasciculus I trans. H. Kohn and revised by the author, published University of Calcutta, 1959.

The Wujra Soochi or Refutation of the Arguments upon which the Brahmanical Institution of Caste is Founded, by the Learned Boodhist Ashwa Ghoshu, trans. B. H. Hodgson. Calcutta: 1839.

INDEX